the Magic Word

Also by Frederick Houk Borsch

The Son of Man in Myth and History

The Christian and Gnostic Son of Man

God's Parable

Introducing the Lessons of the Church Year

Coming Together in the Spirit

Proclamation 2 • Advent Christmas A *(with Davie Napier)*

Proclamation 3 • Pentecost C1

Proclamation 4 • Epiphany A

Power in Weakness

Anglicanism and the Bible (ed.)

Jesus: The Human Life of God

Many Things in Parables

The Bible's Authority in Today's Church *(ed.)*

Christian Discipleship and Sexuality

Outrage and Hope:
A Bishop's Reflections in Times of Change and Challenge

To Dennis

may the magic word fill your life and

the Magic Word

STIRRINGS AND STORIES
OF FAITH AND MINISTRY

Frederick H. Borsch

FREDERICK HOUK BORSCH

CATHEDRAL CENTER PRESS
LOS ANGELES

Cathedral Center Press (an imprint of the Episcopal Diocese of Los Angeles)
P. O. Box 512164, Los Angeles, CA 90051

Unless the author has made his own translation, scripture quotations are from the New Revised Standard Version Bible, copyright 1989, Division of Christian Education of the National Council of the Churches of Christ in the United States of America, U.S.A., and are used by permission.

Cataloging-in-Publication Data
Borsch, Frederick Houk.
    The Magic Word: Stirrings and Stories of Faith and
    Ministry / Frederick Houk Borsch
       p.   cm.
    ISBN 0-9716255-0-6 (pbk. : alk, paper)
    1. Episcopal Church. Diocese of Los Angeles —
    History — 20th, 21st centuries. 2. Church and
    social problems — California — Los Angeles Region.
    3. Los Angeles Region(Calif.) — Church history —
    20th, 21st centuries. 4. Borsch, Frederick Houk.
    I. Title.

Printed in the United States of America

for Matthew Shepard,
for the hotel workers,
for the mothers in prison
and their children

CONTENTS

3   JESUS IS HERE AND OTHER MINISTRIES

Exploding planes and terrorized death, living wage, work and energy, individualism and life lived together, family and sexuality, a worldly Bible and hymn for healing, wiggling one's toes: these are among the topics of the essays and reflections, poems and op-ed pieces written over the last six or so years of life and ministry as bishop of the Episcopal Diocese of Los Angeles. Several of the pieces appeared in the *Los Angeles Times* and other newspapers. Some were written for magazines or journals or special occasions. Many of them were part of my regular musings and communications with the church people of this complex and so diverse region in an effort to think together about significant issues of life and faith. While there is an immediacy and topicality about a number of the writings, the questions and problems, the hopes and fears addressed will long be with us.

The Magic Word is in these ways a companion volume to *Outrage and Hope* (Trinity Press International, 1996) which reflected on earthquakes and riots, fires and floods, evangelism and the environment — things that happened in the earlier years of ministry here — along with a number of other issues that continue on in the present volume. How are people to have hope and faith in a world where bad things happen to every kind of people? What can we do about some of the more trenchant problems facing our world? How can we sometimes laugh and sometimes cry as people struggling and trying to live and love together? The questions and the hopes go on.

I am grateful to Bob Williams and Michelle de la Rosa who helped me edit these pieces, to Janet Wylie who typed and commented on many of them, to Sergio Maldonado who formatted early drafts of this collection, and to Laura Fisher Smith who rendered the design for the text and cover of this book. Most of all I am indebted to colleagues and companions in life and ministry: to Dick Gillett, the people of Project New Hope, and our Urban Interns, among those whose questions and hopes prompted these reflections. I think, too, of Matthew Shepard, the hotel workers, the mothers in prison, the children, and all others who made me pray and ponder and write *The Magic Word* and more.

❖ 1 ❖

New Time Now
and
Times Between

New Time Now

'Stay alert!' "Keep awake!" "Make straight the paths!" "Prepare the way!" These biblical admonitions of renewal, judgment and expectation are heard each December as the church year begins. Similar words were heard as the year 2000 was ushered in: A new age is beginning! Watch out for the Y2K bug! Get things straight!

We survived 2000 all right, and now we are at the beginning of the new millennium—a good time to think about time and the course of human life. The biblical imagery points to a time of consummation and change—or end and new beginning—when the meaning of life is revealed. Then the kingdom of God will be known. The whole creation can be involved in this change. Along with earthquakes, plagues and famine, there are signs in the heavens. The sun will be darkened and the moon will not give its light. The vision becomes a song: "My Lord, what a morning; my Lord, what a morning, when the stars begin to fall."

Cartoons have recently focused only on the ending of this age. The sandwich boards on the bearded prophet proclaimed that "The end is near." Then we were told how four New York newspapers would handle the story. "The World Is to End," would lead *The New York Times* in its major front page column. "See Section B, page 5, for details." "The End of the World Has Come," *The Wall Street Journal* would inform its readers: "Markets to Close Early." "It's Over!" would banner *The New York Post* across its front page. "The World to End," would instruct *The Village Voice*; "Women and Children to Suffer Most."

But, in fact, the secular world with its view of time didn't believe any of it. There would be no great change. Secular time has become a nearly endless stream. Born with the creation of the solar system and before that from some unimaginable big bang, it will continue to the death of our sun and then on to an end of the universe either in fire or in ice. Meanwhile many things happen, but, in the larger perspective, much does not change. Things go on and on. The future, as secular time has it, is much like the present, only longer.

This linear understanding of time actually evolved from the biblical approach that had, in its turn, transformed an earlier cyclical view of life. In earlier ages, time was often viewed as repeating itself in great cycles. The ordered, habitable world — sometimes pictured as a garden — was always tending to wind down toward a chaos from which it then needed to be renewed, same as before. The biblical idea of judgment broke open this cyclical view and flung the garden to the beginning of time with its counterpart as another garden at time's consummation. In Christian faith, there is a third garden — that of Gethsemane, which through suffering and self-giving helps to bring on new life and the new day.

Having given up on judgment, the secular worldview, influenced by tremendous expansions in our understandings of space and time — stretched linear time out behind and before. Any hope now was invested in the idea of progress. In this century just past — which has seen scientific and technological marvels by means of which we now communicate, process information, travel and extend the human life span — such a faith in progress may often have seemed not unreasonable. On the other hand, the century past has been soaked in terrible wars and genocide. If persons alive in 1900 could be transported to this day, they would be amazed to see what we are capable of making, having and knowing, while saddened to realize that human sympathy, kindness and generosity continue to be so fragile. So many goods, they might observe, with little or no growth in the common good.

While yet looking for technological fixes, hope now seems to have turned into worry about the environment, disease, overpopulation, a loss of human dignity in the midst of so much consumption (a kind of technological "affluenza"), and wondering whether life has any meaning at all. "Progress might have been all right once," suggested Ogden Nash, "but it has gone on far too long." There may be individual accomplishments, but hope recedes and a kind of stoic view pervades. Life, as Satchel Paige intimated, is like baseball: "Some days you win; some days you lose; and some days you get rained out."

And now, in our post-modern world, we have even come to a questioning of the significance of our understandings of time itself. Like literary texts, time is deconstructed. It is only, some would contend, what we make of it. It all depends on perspectives, which, of course, in another perspective, is exactly what Einstein told us about the warping of space and time and time's relativity. Time, as regarded in quantum mechanics, is still less linear and more foldable and fungible. It can be seen to bend all sorts of ways, leading to ideas about 10 or 11 dimensional worlds with only four of them part of our direct experience. There might even be more than one dimension of time.

In an experiential sense, we know something about how time seems bendable in everyday life. When we are having a really good time, we look at our watches and say, "I can't imagine where the time went." When we are in the dentist's chair, 45 minutes may seem all day long.

In interesting ways, such views about time's relativity have something in common with biblical prespectives. There we often find more concern with moments in time and their connection than with duration. This has sometimes been called *kairos* time (from the Greek word for "opportunity") as opposed to *kronos* time measured by clock and calendar.

What is *kairos* or opportunity time? A story is told about the philosopher-teacher Paul Tillich whose efforts to explain such matters in English heavily accented with his native German sometimes went right past his students. One day, the story goes, Tillich was taken from his home at the Union Theological Seminary in New York City to Yankee Stadium. There he was made to watch a baseball game that he seemed to find interminable and difficult to understand. Finally, however, it was the top half of the ninth with the Yankees leading 4-3. But the opponents had the bases loaded with only one out when one of their batters hit a sharp ground ball between first and second. Ranging far to his left Bobby Richardson got a glove on it and rifled it over to Kubek who then threw just in time to Collins on first. Tillich jumped on to his seat and, waving his hat in the air, shouted, "Kairos, kairos, kairos!"

In opportunity time, there are decisive times and times of decision —

times which must be seized upon. In other words, there is judgment. Judgment may sometimes seem like a harsh word, but it is the possibility of judgment that brings hope to our world. A world without judgment is a world without discernment between good and evil, between caring and cruelty, between fairness and fatalism. A world without judgment is a world in which nothing matters — in which there would be no story.

In opportunity time, there are moments of significance; an occasion is found for the dots to become connected. They become part of a story — God's great story of creation which involves the chaotic and the ordered, choice and necessity, the conservation, innovation and selectivity of evolution, the dawning of human self-awareness and moral choice, love, mystery and memory, suffering, compassion and new opportunity. Our stories of agony and caring, of grace and growth, are made up of moments linked together more like poetry than mere chronicle. They become part of the story of the context of all life—the divine Awareness of the universe.

This is a drama of significant times and decisive opportunities when what Jesus called the kingdom of God — God's reign — God's ways — become known, indeed, have already begun.

These are the surprising ways in which the humble of spirit are blessed as are those who hunger and thirst for righteousness. Those who make peace and show mercy are to be happy. The fruit of the Spirit of all life is kindness, gentleness, faithfulness, generosity, patience and self-control. In this time, people grow beyond selfishness toward a true maturity of human life. People choose who and whose they will be in life's greatest adventure. This is the intent of the universal drama, in which God's time is bendable, too. In God's perspective, with all-merciful eyes, God sees not only who we are and have been, but who we will be. In this time, from out of the time of our often chaotic and suffering world — even from death, come new opportunity, a new age, a new world.

No doubt, now as then, people would say to Jesus, "Jesus, what do you mean? How could God's ways even now be part of our life? How could the new age be already begun when there is so much that is wrong in the world?" And Jesus responds with story after story. The kingdom is like the treasure hidden in the field. It is the pearl of great price — worth everything you have. It is leaven in the meal. It is like a mustard seed — the tiniest of seeds planted in the ground of life. In the face of so much selfishness, suffering and wrong, it may seem impossibly small. The birds of the air, the searing sun, the thorns and thistles will all work against these seeds. But if you have eyes to see and ears to hear, you will see, and you will begin to live by God's ways. "Thy kingdom come on earth as it is in heaven."

Still today you can hear that hope and expectation almost breathless in Jesus' teaching. "The kingdom of God has drawn near." God's ways are so close that they are already bringing new possibility into our lives.

When teaching students, I would try to give them some sense of how the face of time might be wound up in this manner. "Christmas is coming," I would remind them. Oh, I know it is still weeks away. And we are not supposed to observe it until the 12 days of Christmas. But, even a month away, it is already beginning to change our lives — our holiday plans, how we will spend our time, our money. It affects our spirits. We may even begin to hum its melodies. Or I would say, "Do you remember the test scheduled for a week from Tuesday? I've changed my mind. It will be this Tuesday." "You can't do that," they would complain. "We'll tell the Dean."

But, for a few moments, I had them. By telling them that their time of testing was nearer than they at first believed, I had forced them to begin changing their plans. "Maybe I'd better skip going to the movies. Maybe I'd better get my notes out and read those chapters."

God's ways are near to you, Jesus tells us. You may already participate in the ways of sharing and love. You may already begin to live in the new age. At any moment, it may break into your lives, in times of great friendship, of love flooding in, of mercy and forgiveness, of courage and beauty, of servant ministry and sharing with others. It will not always be joy. It will be testing, too. Sometimes you will think the ways of hungering for fairness, showing mercy and trying to make peace are pointless. Some days your own self-centeredness and anxiety about others getting more than you will mount up. Some days evil and suffering will seem to overwhelm so that you may even think it is smart to give up trying to advocate for, support and mentor all our young people. You may wish you could stop striving to overcome oppression and the humiliation of others in poverty or racism.

But, know this, the God who is the divine Awareness of all life — the Abba who is like a caring parent to all people — this God stays in covenant through evil and suffering. Pain and wrong are part of creation, and God takes them on, so that what happens to us, also happens to God. Despite all their power and life's tragedies, God remains faithful, giving us the hope and courage to carry on in God's ways. Amid the color and pageantry, the drama and heartbreak of this creation, the story of divine love goes forward.

Paul put it rather like this: "It appears to me that whatever we suffer now will show up only dimly when compared to the wonders God has in store for us. It is as though all creation is standing on tiptoe longing to see an unforgettable vision, the children of God being born into wholeness.

"Although creation is unfinished, still in the process of being born, it carries within a secret hope. And the hope is this: A day will come when we will be rescued from the pain of our limitations and incompleteness and be given our share in a freedom that can only belong to the children of God.

"At the present moment all creation is struggling as though in the pangs of childbirth. And that struggling creation includes even those of us who have had a taste of the Spirit. We peer into the future with our limited vision; unable to see all that we are destined to be, yet believing because of a hope we carry so deep within."

So stay awake! Keep alert! Prepare the way! We do not know when God's time in its fruition comes, but we know something of what it is like because the kingdom of God — God's ways — have already drawn near. For a people of hope and of faith the new age wakes; God's ways inbreak, and the new time has begun.

The Magic Word

I can speak with some authority about being a child since I once was one. I imagine that you were too. Do you remember how, when we were kids, we loved magic words? With "shazam" we and Billy Batson could turn ourselves into Captain Marvel and maybe other such marvelous heroes. By saying "abracadabra" we could make things appear or disappear. We wanted a magic word that could make things change or at least appear differently.

And maybe that hope never does go completely away. Some of us carry it into adult life with beliefs like those of alchemy or astrology or maybe Technology with a capital "T." Some people say that a lot of religion is based on fantasy and magical thinking, and that could well seem the case when you listen to the logic of some of our prayers which seems to be that two and two should never be four. And speaking of numbers, in these so modern days, the magic words for a good portion of the population — the words which would seem able to change everything — might be something like seven, eleven, nineteen, twenty-six, thirty-two with mega ten.

Then I remember an older sister teasing, "You can't have it until you say the magic word. Say the magic word." And finally I would want that piece of candy or gum enough so that I would purse out that word "please." Later I would learn and teach my own children that there is a pleasantness and helpfulness about the word please. It can make life go more smoothly. But I don't think that this really qualifies it to be a magic word. For one thing, most of us detect and tend to discount the measure of self-interest that is part of the word please. It almost always asks for something, and there is rarely anything surprising or magical about that.

No, I think that the magic word comes on the other side of human events, as it were, and need not be asking for anything. That word is "thanks." Archbishop William Temple held that "It is more important to thank God for blessings received than to pray for them beforehand. For that forward-looking prayer, though right as an expression of dependence upon God, is still self-centered in part, at least, in its interest; there is something we hope to gain by our prayer. But the backward-looking act of Thanksgiving is quite free from this. In itself it is quite selfless. This is akin to love."

Now you may be saying that the only magic going on here is my trickery in trying to convince you that there really is such a thing as a magical word when, now that we are all grown-up, we know that life doesn't really have any magic words. But let me in turn ask you to search your own memory, honestly and quite realistically. Remember our criterion is the capacity of a word to change the way things appear. Let's go even further. Let's ask that our magic word not only change the way things look, but also how they really are.

I know it is pretty standard advice, but I trust that more than once in your life, when feeling sorry for yourself — trapped in a slough of self-pity and maybe edging into despair — you remembered to count your blessings and say thanks. That may sound to some like only a sentimental trick, but if one really puts some gratitude into the thought, it is amazing how it can transform circumstances. Meister Eckhart maintained that "if the only prayer you say in your whole life is 'Thank you,' that would suffice," and I believe he is right — not only because our gratitude is pleasing to God, but because of the kind of persons thanks makes of us.

More amazing still is what the magic word can do to an angry person. Just as powerfully as any comic book word, I have seen the magic word stop enraged people dead in their tracks. I once was furious with a colleague — so angry with the way he had treated me that I wanted my words to be daggers. That emotion, of course, usually only makes others angry too, but in this case my colleague said, "Thanks. I appreciate your pointing that out to me." It took me at least ten seconds to get my next words out, and they were very different words — words turning to friendship and new relationship.

Anger, greed, anxiety, guilt — I find the magic word to be powerful against many of life's demons that want to rule over my life and strangle my capacities for loving and caring. I find I often need to battle envy. Ever since I can remember I have had to struggle with envy and jealousy. Maybe we all do, and this envy flows from a well of insecurity deep within us. In any case, it first was siblings and then classmates and then others who were getting better grades, or more touchdowns, or who were taller, had better looks, more money, better reviews of their books, a more prestigious position. I still surprise myself with the knots I can tie myself into when being jealous of others, and (talk about distorting reality) incredible the way I can then lose sight of the good things in my own life.

The other side of that insecure envy is, of course, the need to cut the object of my jealousy down to size. "Well, maybe his book got great reviews, but he's not a very good teacher." "Maybe she's a pretty important person, but she only got there because she is so ambitious." And, given the opportunity, that urge to diminish others can well break forth in gossip — you know, all that supposedly harmless chatting about others that may for a little while soothe jealousy and insecurity, but still leaves the taste of bitterness.

What I am in the process of learning is the magic power of thanks to extinguish envy's fiery darts. Sometimes to begin with, I have to think of someone whose accomplishments do not threaten me. Unlike Salieri I am not jealous of Mozart. Obviously that is because he lived in another century and because I am not a musician. The result is that I am purely grateful that he lived and composed so gloriously. I give thanks to God for Mozart. And then I try also to give thanks that Bob is such a fine teacher, that Ralph is such a good leader and makes the rich living he does, and that Betty writes so intelligently about the New Testament. Not only is my relationship with them then changed, but now — wonder of wonders — there are so many things and people in life to give thanks for. What used to make me angry can now make me praise. Grumbling becomes gratitude, and a new community of relationships begins to emerge.

One of the happiest aspects of the Bible is all the thanks and praise it contains: for food, for rain, for sun, for all life's beauty and pageantry, for friends, for compassion. David, with arms upraised before the Lord, rejoices that he is able to offer up so many things and that now, "I have seen thy people, who are present here, offering freely and joyously to you." The psalmist urges that we make a "joyful noise to the Lord" — that we "enter God's gates with thanksgiving." And then there is regular thanksgiving of Paul's letters even when in tribulation and prison. So may we also join with George Herbert when he prays for the magic of thanksgiving.

> *Thou that has given so much to me.*
> *Give one thing more, a grateful heart …*
> *Not thankful, when it pleaseth me,*
> *As if thy blessings hid spare days;*
> *But such a heart, whose pulse may*
>   *be thy praise.*

**AUGUST 6, 1945
A-BOMB DROPPED ON JAPAN!**

August Six

Up there horizon's edge might also be
the great water's shore, with the green river
draining this mountain and turning the plain
before generously making the sea.

Then on morning's wings the three of us
climb with him so far that another shore
is rising on that edge, and with it awe
there is no escaping, nor what we must.

Pray hand holds fast as the skies come open,
when for peace he looses day-star's secret,
falling without other benediction
than the radiance of night now given?

Who could have been known while yet in the womb
if not such humanity, face aglow
and clothes so dazzling white no earth's fuller
could possibly prepare them for this tomb?

Lit from within, the columned cloud ascends,
majestic over us, hiding all presence,
though where does one go, if still at grave's bed
there also thunders "beloved" and sends

Terror on us and any loved dearly
by one for whom night and light could be like,
abandoning in the noonday darkness
his life offering said to be glory?

We may, of course, have been sleeping, a dream,
and it is time to come down from that edge.
The sun has returned, though it is cold now,
with silence only his death can redeem.

Nighty-Night

Now and again I come across one of those go-getters who tell me they begrudge any time wasted in sleep. As much as a third of one's life in bed when there is so much to do and enjoy! Winston Churchill was among those types, staying up half the night, though I am told he often was in bed late into the morning and fell asleep at meetings during the day.

I find sleep to be one of those goods of life like water and air. I only begin really to miss them when they are in short supply.

Recently I went through a period when pain regularly woke me up at night. Sometimes I would have trouble falling back asleep. And then there might well be something to fret about. And one can worry, too, about not getting enough sleep for the day ahead.

At three or four a.m., fears may mount dark horses. Perhaps it is because, lying there lightless, we feel so little in control.

I am reminded of the jest that I and others have used when taking on the responsibilities and surprises of a new job.

"How are you sleeping, Bishop?" a well-wisher inquires.

"Oh, like a baby."

"Really? That's great."

"Yes. I wake up every hour and cry."

Then it is such a blessing when good sleep returns. The body chemicals are back in rested balance. The brain has done some discharging. And "dreaming," I recall a psychiatrist saying, "permits each and every one of us to be quietly and safely insane every night of our lives." Now waking, I yawn, broadly stretch out my arms and give thanks.

There is peace in knowing that, while we have responsibilities, we are yet not wholly in charge. The day has come again without us. Our ultimate peace and trust and rest are in God. In that faith, we may even grow in our slumber. "Those who have the gale of the Holy Spirit," Brother Lawrence held, "go forward even in sleep."

Nor must it always be at night. I don't nap as much as I probably should, but I had a grandfather who rose early to do a full morning's work. At eleven a.m. he went up to his bedroom, got into his pajamas and went to sleep for an hour before lunch. "A nap after lunch is silver," he told this curious grandson, "but a nap before lunch is golden."

I have a walk-in closet into which I go at night to take off my day clothes and put on my pajamas. In there on the wall, where it catches my eye, I have tacked up a bedtime prayer of John XXIII.

There are sure a lot of problems in your Church, Lord.
But they are your problems.
You can handle it. I'm going to bed.

Nighty-night.

Shooters Both

'Yeats saw that out of his quarrel with others man makes rhetoric, but out of his quarrel with himself poetry. Herbert surely had no quarrel with others. What he had was an argument, not with others, nor with himself primarily, but with God; and God always won." This insight of poet R.S. Thomas is manifest in many of George Herbert's poems.

"Artillerie" begins with a startling image.

> As I one ev'ning sat before my cell,
> Me thought a star did shoot into my lap.
> I rose and shook my clothes, as knowing well
> That from small fires comes oft no small mishap.

The undertone of playfulness, which continues through the poem, begins in the absurdly calm manner with which the poet deals with such a fantastic event. He seems almost ready to ignore it. Then Herbert hears a voice speaking to him of his stubbornness and efforts to avoid engagement with God. He continues:

> I, who had heard of music in the spheres,
> But not of speech in stars, began to muse:
> But turning to my God, whose ministers
> The stars and all things are; …

This "speech" which may be an inner voice, but also of God, is part of the dialogical character of many of Herbert's prayer poems. The poet now wills to respond to this "Dread Lord," — the God of all stars and spheres. Yet, although he indicates a partial submission, he also realizes that he has his own artillery with which he can, as it were, return God's fire. His "shooters," his bursting shots and shooting stars, are, however, but his entreaties.

> *But I have also stars and shooters too,*
> *Born where thy servants both artilleries use.*
> *My tears and prayers night and day do woo,*
> *And work up to thee; …*

The prayer warfare remains so uneven, and Herbert more than hints, greatly unfair.

> *Not, but I am (I must say still)*
> *Much more obliged to do thy will,*
> *Than thou to grant mine: …*

Yet he persists and so would God in this mock battle at once absurd and vital. The fight is fixed, but God invites it to continue.

> *Then we are shooters both, and thou dost deign*
> *To enter combat with, and contest*
> *With thine own clay…*

"Ernest prayer," maintained John Donne, "hath the nature of Importunity; We press, we importune God.… Prayer hath the nature of Impudency; We threaten God in Prayer… And God suffers this Impudency, and more."

One may hear, as well, the voice of the psalmist, railing, pleading.

The title of Herbert's poem likely refers to the passage in the letter to the Ephesians which counsels the Christian to "put on the whole armor of God." Here, however, the armor is as much to protect against God as it is to do battle with the powers of evil, though even then, it is God's armor.

Herbert would like to come to some kind of bargain with God.

> *But I would parley fain:*
> *Shun not my arrows, and behold my breast.*

Let my arrows reach you and forget not my humanity, he asks. But God remains champion.

Yet if thou shunnest, I am thine:
I must be so, if I am mine.
There is no articling [bargaining] with thee:
I am but finite, yet thine infinitely.

Herbert's speaker comes to understand something of the mystery of God's sovereignty in ways that remind of God's relationship with Job. In theological terms, the speaker has argued himself into understanding that the unequal terms of the relationship are part of the conditions of being human. He may rebel against those conditions, but God sticks with him through that rebellion so that he may see that the terms, while unfair, are finally the only terms on which God and humans can interact. In the figurative terms of the poem, the speaker resolves to continue the prayerful assaults on God, realizing that it is his good fortune to be destined to be captive even before the first volley has been shot.

God's sovereignty, Herbert intimates, could wipe us out and always threatens to pre-empt us. But there is still God's forbearance — a gracious willingness to stay with us and honor us even when we get it wrong.

Did ever such a star shoot into your lap?

Gun Down a Memory

Place: The young men's locker room of Hinsdale Township High School. Year: 1952. Actors: Lefty Pena, myself and Bobby Schatts. Behind the scenes, a lot was going on. Hinsdale was an elite Chicago suburb. It was segregated. The high school district, however, also encompassed Westmont. In Westmont there lived the sons and daughters of Mexican Americans who had helped build the Burlington Railroad. Lefty was one of them, a senior and a star on the football team. With his jock status and outgoing personality, he could mingle with the rest of us — up to a point, like trying to date the girls from Hinsdale.

I was a junior, and a minor figure on the football team. But I lived in Hinsdale. I was a top student, popular, a class officer and oblivious of my privileges. Bobby was a freshman, a little kid at the time. He was the younger brother of a good-looking girl in my class.

When I walked in to the locker room, Lefty was introducing Bobby to some form of initiation rite that involved holding his head in the toilet while flushing it. I took some exception to this. When I came to, I was sitting in the coach's office. One of the first things I remember was how upset the coach was with me. He liked me, but I had messed with his star athlete.

It all blew over. Lefty came to visit me in the hospital. Lying there with my left cheek bone broken, I realized he had knocked me out with his right hand. A sneak punch!

Years later, Lefty and I met at a retirement party for Coach Dickinson. Lefty was now himself a coach and respected teacher in a neighboring high school. He cried and apologized again, and then we hugged and laughed remembering the incident.

21

And now I think, what if guns had been only a phone call away or easily purchased by a girlfriend at a gun show? What if a gun had been readily available to me or to Lefty or even Bobby Schatts?

Piper City Christmas

My grandfather Houk was an undertaker. He lived in an Illinois farm town some forty miles south of Kankakee and ninety miles south of Chicago. The year my mother, Pearl, was born, six hundred and fifty people lived in Piper City. Only a few more than six hundred and fifty live there now.

My grandfather was the most important person in Piper City. The few other professional people — a doctor, a lawyer and a clergyman — came and went, but Grandfather was there to stay. He had been with many of those families through their toughest times. Although he had only an education through the eighth grade, his advice was sought on lots of matters.

He also owned a furniture store uptown, as they called the little cluster of stores lined up on both sides of the Toledo, Peoria and Western railroad tracks. A generation earlier, an undertaker in similar circumstances might have made his own caskets. Now Ernest Houk sold furniture and caskets.

The caskets, however, were not in the store. They were in the house that was both a residence and a funeral home. Two rooms upstairs had open caskets on display. Downstairs, across from the kitchen, there was a preparation room for the bodies and a hand-drawn elevator to bring the caskets up and down. I thought that elevator was one of the greatest inventions in the world.

Out in back there was a barn. A generation or two earlier a predecessor of my grandfather would have kept a horse-drawn hearse there. Now my grandfather had a big black motor hearse that he used to bring the bodies to the house as well as later to bear them to the cemetery. Sometimes the hearse doubled as an ambulance if there was an accident on one of the nearby highways.

There was also a horse named Toots who belonged to my Aunt Vera. I occasionally got to sit up on Toots and ride him slowly. That, however, was a little scary. I mostly liked to slip out and visit the barn by myself. I would examine the shiny hearse and sit on a hay bale and smell the barn while watching Toots chew and shuffle around.

I remember the barn and the house as being huge. My older sister tells me this isn't so. Maybe the rooms were not as large as a small boy recollects, but there were a lot of them. There had to have been at Christmastime when we came to visit with my two sisters. Usually my two aunts and uncles and five cousins had already arrived. Sometimes we were so crowded that I slept on a cot outside one of the rooms with the empty caskets. I don't think that ever bothered me. I may have thought that a lot of grandfathers were undertakers.

Downstairs there was a living room and a kind of large middle parlor and still another room behind that. We ate Christmas dinner in the middle parlor, but sometimes around Christmas, and especially when I visited my grandparents during the summer, there would be a body laid out in the middle parlor. From time to time there might even be another one in its casket in the rear room. Often the funeral services were held in the middle parlor. I remember in the summer the folks sitting there on folding chairs looking sad and hot, whispering and fanning themselves with fans that said "E. H. Houk Funeral Home."

There could be long stretches, however, when no one was in that parlor except the body in its casket with the top half propped open. It was so quiet and mysterious I could not help but be drawn in, a solemn-faced boy, sometimes stepping quite near and gazing at the dead face, hands folded on its chest. Once in a while it would be a younger person. One time, I remember, it was a child, and that did scare me. But for the most part, the bodies looked very old. They lay on their satin pillows to make them appear comfortable, but I wasn't fooled. The casket must have been very hard beneath them, and, despite my aunt's cosmetic efforts, they seemed very dead to me. My younger sister was scared they would move, but I knew they never would. I knew that Grandfather had drained the blood out of them and pumped in formaldehyde and water.

I wondered what had happened to them. I wondered what it was like to be alive and then to be dead. I wondered how they had died. I wondered where they were now. The grownups said they were at peace.

I was pretty sure that under the half of the casket that was closed they didn't have any shoes on. What would be the point? I kind of wondered why they wasted putting their good clothes on them. Some of them had their glasses on too. A few times I came so close that I touched them, putting my hand on their foreheads. It was like putting my hand on a cold stone. I discovered that if you pushed on the nostrils of a dead person they would stay in. I don't imagine I was allowed to do that more than once.

We usually arrived on Christmas Eve about suppertime. Excited as we were about Christmas and seeing each other, after supper we soon fell into the deep sleep of kids. But the next morning it was quickly one-up-all-up. We eyed the presents under the tree, making our guesses and tantalizing one another if we thought we knew what someone else was getting that year.

Aunt Vera played the piano and we sang. Some of the songs didn't have anything to do with Christmas: "You Are My Sunshine" and "Twinkle, Twinkle Little Star," though I suppose one could think of that as the star of Bethlehem.

The waiting seemed forever. Grandfather would go up to the furniture store to have coffee with his cronies and probably Christmas schnapps as well. There could be no Christmas dinner until he came home. We also knew that in his pockets, he had shiny silver dollars for each of us cousins.

We would take turns running to the corner to see if we could spot him coming. He always had his gray fedora hat on his rather square head. He was a taciturn man. I do not remember his ever saying much to me, although he did teach me how to play checkers with the strategy of making kings early. I loved stacking up a king, and in each new game I was sure I was going to beat him, until he would devastate me out of nowhere with a double or even triple jump.

On Christmas morning I think I felt angry with him, making us wait like that. And, when he did come, it seemed as if he were laughing at us. Years later I learned that he had been waiting up at the store for Grandmother to call and say that dinner was ready. All along it was

Grandmother, born Minnie Mabel Munson, but whom the grandkids called Momo, who was the one making us do the waiting.

But then the meal appeared in all its steaming glory: wonderful mashed potatoes one could make into a mound with a hole in the middle for the gravy and to float a few peas in. This came along with the turkey and dressing and was followed by the pumpkin pie and a big dab of whipped cream. It was Thanksgiving all over again.

Too soon we had torn into all the presents, played with the ones that weren't clothes, and taken a few out into the frigid late afternoon where one's breath could be seen as puffs of air the cold wind blew away. Sometimes there was a fight with a cousin, and afterwards, tired and with feelings I couldn't sort out, I might sneak off and watch Toots snort and shuffle around as the last shafts of winter sunlight slid away, and it began to grow dark in the barn.

There were several things I think I was beginning to learn on those Christmases. The first had to do with the waiting. Waiting can be hard, but it can also help sort things out. There can be an attentive waiting that is not just not doing anything. It is something like being a bird watcher. It is a way of being. One sees things that otherwise might not be noticed. One learns to appreciate. I laugh to remember that, because of its initials, the Toledo, Peoria and Western railroad was also known as Take Patience and Walk. I have more than a hunch that the people who lived in Piper City in those days had something to teach me about waiting and patience.

I later came to realize that there is a considerable amount of waiting in the Bible: for children, for escape from slavery in Egypt, for the promised land, for the prophet, for return from exile, for wisdom, for rebuilding the holy city and temple, for the messiah, for the kingdom of God, for God's presence. And there is a lot of waiting in our lives: for Christmas, to grow up, for a career, for love, perhaps to be married, for children, for success, to be wiser, to be mature, to retire, for a diagnosis, for the meaning and value of life. None of these ever arrive perfectly, but in careful waiting one may come to see what might most be worth waiting for.

A second thing I think I began to understand is that good things can happen in small ways. At Christmas time we sang "O Little Town of

Bethlehem" and retold the story of the tiny baby in the manger. There were also angels singing from on high and wise men coming from afar, but one could not miss the point of the apparent insignificance of it all in that stable in out-of-the-way Bethlehem. It makes me think still of the barn and house in little Piper City and the ways Christmas came to us there.

There was something solemn about those Christmases too. One Christmas, the door off the middle parlor to the rear room was shut because someone was "at rest" there. Another Christmas night, after all the children were finally in bed, I heard Grandfather back the hearse down the driveway to go out into the darkness on one of those necessary errands of his.

When I was older, I learned that in the church calendar the day after Christmas is Saint Stephen's Day when the church remembers its first martyr who was stoned to death. Two days later is called Holy Innocents, the commemoration of all the little ones King Herod was said to have slaughtered when he was trying to kill the baby Jesus. We remember as well all the children killed in war or by human cruelty and indifference. In Piper City, I was already beginning to understand that Christmas does not come apart from tears. The deepest meaning of the joy of "God is with us" — of Emmanuel — would have to happen in that home with its caskets and presents, all my relatives and the bodies at rest, Toots and the hearse, the feasting and love and sobbing.

Solos and Solidarity: Individualism and Our Common Life

Baccalaureate Address: University of Southern California
May, 1997

It is a privilege to be with you at this time of commencement and to join in gratitude for your achievements and graduation from this distinguished University. And now I want also to join in that chorus of voices asking you, "What's next?" You may, indeed, be a little tired of relatives and friends posing that question and now just answer it off-handedly in terms of where you are going to live or what your job will be or where you are going to graduate school. Or perhaps your reply is that for the moment you are keeping your options open.

But I mean something more far reaching by the question, and I know that some part of you is also asking — not only what will be your work or profession, but what kind of life will you have. We might speak of it as vocation — some sense of calling and purpose in life. It is part of that big, "What's it all about?" "What's it all for?" question.

Like you I read novels and I go to movies. I listen to people talk about their lives. Sometimes I hear them reflect about what is missing. What seems to make them most sad in the final analysis is not some lack of money, or even of health and love. Whatever precise words they use, what a number of people say they miss most — or still wish and hope for in their lives is a sense of purpose, of belonging to and contributing — of making a difference — sharing something of lasting value.

I know that may seem to run counter to some of the received wisdom or at least the cynical wisdom of our time which one can hear in this story of a proposal of marriage. "Dearest," the young man said, "I'm not wealthy like Howard Brown. I don't own a Mercedes, two homes and a yacht like he does, but I love you very much, and I want to marry you." The young woman thought for a moment and then responded, "Darling, I love you, too, but tell me more about Howard Brown."

I'm told that a survey of a number of Americans was done a few years ago asking them how they might fulfill their potential. This was no easy question, but one might have expected, or at least hoped, that a number of the answers would have been along the lines of, "I would be a better person," and, "I would try to do more for others." But "better person" did not even finish in the rankings. The top two answers were, "I want to be rich" and "I want to be thin."

One doesn't have to condemn the desire to have means in this life and to be attractive to still be afraid that, if these are the dominant aspirations of our people, the American dream has somehow become a kind of nightmare of self-absorbed individuals easily subject to all the whims and whiles of consumerism.

Wendell Berry set the warning to poetry:

Love the quick profit,
the annual raise,
Vacation with pay. Want more
of everything ready-made.
Be afraid
To know your neighbors
and to die.
And you will have a window in your head.
Not even your future will be a mystery anymore.
Your mind will be punched in a card
And shut away in a little drawer.
When they want you to buy something,
They will call you.
When they want you to die for profit,
They will let you know.

Or, as it has been put more succinctly, "People all wrapped up in themselves make pretty small packages."

There is plenty of evidence around us as well that lives driven by the motivations of wealth and appearance are frequently anxious lives, caught by fears about not enough, or of someone else having more, suffering from various types of addictions, all too often lonely.

More than two decades ago Bob Dylan saw what the spirit of the age could be leading to when he wrote and sang:

> *There are those who worship loneliness,*
> *I'm not one of them.*
> *In this age of fiberglass*
> *I'm looking for a gem.*

What might that gem be? If we are looking for more than material-ism and what consumerism seems to offer in life, what is it that we are hoping for, longing for, dreaming of? What would be that less anxious, more fulfilled self — not a false self, but what we would like to think of as our truer and more mature selves — what the poet John Donne once called our *abler* self.

Often today we may hear the lyrics of that song of hope in the words, "Be all that you can be." Or the words may be heard in the challenges to individual excellence and self-fulfillment. And surely these are worthy goals here — to be the best chemist, or carpenter, or business leader, or doctor, or musician, or lawyer, or gardener, or micro-biologist, or teacher and scholar you can be — to achieve well in one's profession.

Yet, even if we do achieve in these ways, we could well find that there is something missing in our lives — a place of emptiness, exacerbated and made more lonely if we also find that we must do our achieving a high state of competitiveness with others.

Increasingly in our society, the political and even ethical language of values seems built on a rhetoric of liberal libertarianism. It is heard throughout the political spectrum, more often in terms of individual and group rights on the liberal left, and of economic rights on the neo-con-servative but also liberal right wing of our politics. It is as though the only values held in common are those which allow for each person to be as unencumbered as possible. Built upon an understanding of each individ-ual as an emancipated volunteerist persona, the goal seems to be, as one interpreter expressed it, that all would maximize their opportunities to be "free to choose and adopt a lifestyle which allows expression of their uniqueness and individuality."

The role of government, thus, becomes to leave us as free as possible to do this. The ensurer of our rights, the state is to be as neutral as possible, bracketing any other questions of morality or what is good for us to accomplish as a people. Indeed, there is often considerable hostility to government should it be thought to have any other role than that of guaranteeing our personal freedoms.

In all this there has been gain, in diversity, in opportunities to develop and achieve, in keeping people free from a tyranny of views and attitudes of a majoritarian conformity. Yet one sees the down side, too — such as fear of having some goods and values in common, the increasing difficulty of sustaining discussion about these common goods, other than as if individual rights were the only goal.

When we today worry about the breakdown of the family and are concerned about family values, we must recognize that it is this making a goal of the freedom of each individual for his or her own unencumbered self-expression which is also making it so hard for individuals to make and keep commitments, driving up divorce rates and parental absenteeism. It is why we find so much self-absorption and preoccupation, ironically leaving many so readily open to manipulation by a consumerist mentality and skilled media. "Be all that you can be" becomes "You deserve a break today" with self-identity found in what is bought and owned, again ironically, often turning out to be what the Joneses already have.

There is irony, and perhaps some paradox, too, in the recognition that the self-government upon which our liberties depend, can only be maintained with some vision of our being a people together, a willingness to give of ourselves, to be ready to be mutually responsible for the sake of the civic enterprise and to build up the social capital of cooperation.

An obvious example has to do with our care for our environment. More than eighty percent of the voters in the United States when polled say, "Environmental standards cannot be too high" and that improvement must be made "regardless of cost." We recognize that it is in our own self-interest to keep from seriously degrading our air and water and natural habitats and places of recreation. Yet, because individual and small group interests are often more affected by particular decisions and actions than the common good, and because of a fear of limiting the rights of individuals to do whatever they want with their own, the environment continues to receive more lip service than help.

It is still more difficult to give serious discussion to concerns for the environment of poorer persons and neighborhoods, of other countries, of our children, much less of other species. One commentator noted how ironic it would be if human beings, with their intelligence and awareness making them the sole moral species, acted only in self-interest toward all the rest. "Ought not this sole moral species do something less self-interested than count all the products of an evolutionary ecosystem as rivets in their spaceship, resources in their larder, laboratory materials, recreation for their ride?"

On the one hand, it is good that we live in a society which values and protects individual rights and respects individual achievement, along with responsibility for taking care of oneself and also, we always hope, some responsibility for protecting the rights of others. But can that be the whole story of the human adventure?

Many business leaders — who otherwise espouse a totally free market, even a kind of social Darwinism — are also aware that their own companies do not run well with unrestrained internal competition, each person only out for oneself. They come to value employees who have learned a sense of teamwork, how to enter into a common enterprise — to look out for each other. In many areas of life, in business, in families, on teams, in mountain climbing, in neighborhoods, in hospitals, in universities, there is great value in a sense of interdependence as well as independence.

"If I am not for myself, who will be? But if I am only for myself, who am I?" a rabbi once asked. A willingness to share, to use our achievements for others as well as ourselves, being glad for the good that comes to others, not wanting to put others down so we can go up over them, having the imagination, empathy and compassion to put oneself in other's shoes: not wanting others to be humiliated in life by lack of food, lack of medical care, lack of educational opportunity, lack of a job, not insisting on living at the center of life, not making all decisions solely on the basis of one's own benefit: these are the signs of character, of a maturity of person. Many people of Africa speak of *ubuntu* — the realization that our full humanity is known in relationship with the humanity of others and in life for the community and for others.

"Love your neighbor as yourself." There are people who will tell you that this is impossible. That humans are from birth and onward too self-centered to experience such love. But there are resources in the religious traditions and in contemporary communities of faith that say that individuals and communities of people can at least begin to know such mature love, that they can, as Martin Buber interpreted it, begin "to love one's neighbor as someone like oneself." They recognize that the understanding of freedom which can only prize being able to do what I want to do when I want to do it, can be a form of enslavement to being able to only what I want to do when I want to do it. Human self-centeredness is seen as a kind of sickness, manifesting itself in loneliness and anxiety, worries about not getting enough, leading to jealousy, anger and forms of addiction, sometimes to alcohol and drugs or sex, sometimes to work, or constantly searching for distraction in entertainment, television, music, anything which might ease the anxiety, sometimes the self-pity — but never enough.

The effects of these anxieties and addictions accumulate in the larger society — family or clan anxiously caring only for itself, suspicious, fearful, prejudiced against those who are different, racism, sexism, gross economic disparity, and the humiliation of others through their lack of opportunity, and respect.

But there can be healing in prayer and worship, in caring for others. There can be a kind of purity of heart — a simplicity of intention in life — the beginning of a cure for always thinking one is busy, a cure which comes through a sense of priority, a sense of what's most important. One can find the beginning of that peace through faith in the Divine Spirit, the source and destiny of all our lives, in whom we live and move and have our being, in which we can know ourselves valued and given our dignity — each one of us equally so.

I'd like to think that this purity of heart is the gem Bob Dylan sings about. Jesus says it is discovered as the pearl of great price recognized in those virtues which will always seem contrarian in a world without a faith greater than the self. Blessed are the humble and those who hunger and thirst for righteousness; blessed are the merciful, the pure in heart, the peace makers. In story after story Jesus radically questions the propensity to try to gain advantage over others, not least by using religion and a sense of relationship with God for a sense of superiority — by setting others aside in a competition of gamesmanship.

You will, we hope, do many great things in life. We who this day are your friends and mentors, family members and admirers of your accomplishments and achievements wish that you will do very well in life. The chief hope for true greatness, for maturity and even heroism in the human adventure is that you will have care for others, that you will through your achievements give of yourselves, that you will generously help build families and communities, work places and institutions of character and mutuality, of solidarity with one another,

There is an old proverb from India: "All is lost unless it is given." We will be best remembered in life, not for what we have, but what have shared with others and given away. That's the opposite of that yuppie idea that the one who dies with the most toys wins.

Probably on your own or in some religion or philosophy class you have come up against what is called the problem of evil. Why is there so much wrong and evil in the world? How can there be a God of rightness and mercy and love with all that is wrong and painful?

Yet there is another problem — one which we might call the problem of good. Why are not people only self-centered and self-absorbed? Why do almost all people at least sometimes aspire to do something more? Why and how are there some who become mature enough to care more consistently for others and for the common good? There is a sense even of a kind of mystery — that the more we share of ourselves the more we will have, that love and caring do require sacrifice and even suffering but that then we also participate in what life can be most about? Where does this kind of greatness and heroism come from?

Another rabbi once said that each of us has four songs to sing: a song of the self, a song of the people, a song of all humanity, and a song of the cosmos. Solos will enrich this music but there is a greater music. Nor is this one song to be intoned in unison. Rather it is a chorus in harmony — a complex motet in which we all are invited to sing and play — to share of ourselves in college and class, in family and neighborhood, in our community and society, at work and at play, in prayer and in worship, in individual and common achievement. This is the musical gem — the *ubuntu* music which will make you and us all most fully human.

It is in appreciation and awe for the beauty and richness of this music that we are met this evening to share of ourselves and to give our thanks and praise to the Spirit of all life, now and always.

The Storm

A few gusts at first, a bit of huffing,
coming from the east it might have blown past,
but soon the waves darkened, and lashing about
and around our slight craft, began washing
over the gunwales and pitching the mast,
wearing us out, in heart-wrenching dips and swaths.

And there lofting his gaping mouth again
was that beast, Leviathan, the monster
from the depths of all our fears, made for sport,
you say, but for us terror-struck the end
would come, while astern whom we call master
slept, legs athwart, on that damn cushion of his.

He rests, while we like drunken sailors lurch
and in panic sicken it is chaos
that triumphs over all our good and games,
of hope and fear, of both/and, the search
among propensities for that not lost
with all our names to the grim and grinning one.

Bailing madly, we shout at it and him:
"Don't you care that we perish? Rouse yourself,
if you are he who you say you are, Lord."
So now lifting himself off his cushion,
in peace he creates both sea and wind still,
and all restored, asks of what we are afraid.

The Flood

The other day a man I barely knew
said he'd seen my blue canoe,
stored downside up – bow moored in a tree.
Smiling at my clergy collar, he asked
if I knew something he ought note?
whether he too should buy a boat?

I started to return his bandy
before a crafty vision stole my eyes,
for sometimes I do see the river rising,
coursing white ribbed, then pooled and gliding,
down which we may escape.

I did not mean to bemuse his smile
by looking so far away,
but what was I to say?

Sturgeon Narrows

Not only twice, young man and older now,
but more than forty years I've fished this stream,
swum it cold and fathomed pools and currents,
not all summers, but enough to have seen
a brown bear when we surprised each other
as she swiped fish among the rocks just where
the waters shallow clear and rush so well
that only strong arms can come cross it here.

Those friends and wife and sons have paddled with
and against the steady, moving river.
We have drunk and fed from it, while hearing
its ongoing passage with each other.

Another time alone above its draw
I lured a pike whose instinct knew the stream
a place to tug the canoe in again
and again, 'til I caught him tired and clean.

Although a birch has fallen in the bend,
it looks unchanged, the river stepped into
first those years ago, having read time's truth:
this is other water, each time anew.

Stepping again, I feel the cold, but sense
as well water flowing age upon age,
here and there, for all others, gone to come
what yet goes on among enduring change.
I see the bear and feel the pulling pike,
looking up and down the river, its same
shaped flux, forever changing, cold and bright,
as this foot has its place within the stream.

Processions I Have Known

Some of the best, of course, have been on Palm Sunday, though I am never sure how to hold my face in those parades of such mixed emotions. Marching about with our banners, crosses and torches, occasionally being whacked in the face by someone turning too fast with a palm branch over their shoulder, we sing "All Glory, Laud and Honor" and "Ride On, Ride On in Majesty" as we remember the kingly one hailed while entering Jerusalem. Soon, however, he will be betrayed in the same city, deserted by those who cheered for him and crucified.

I've wondered, too, whether that first Palm Sunday was as elaborate as sometimes imagined. Maybe the crowd wasn't all that large. Perhaps there were a few logistical problems with donkeys and branches strewn in procession for a king soon to be slapped and spit upon. It had to have been ironic by the standards of worldly power, more like a mock opera.

When I was Dean of the Princeton University Chapel, a cathedral-like church in the heart of that campus, I set about converting the largely Presbyterian and other protestant-type Sunday morning worshippers to a few more richly liturgical ways. One of these was the Palm Sunday procession. Outside around the Chapel we would go before entering the main doors and heading up the long center aisle. I was also eager on this day to make use of the outdoor pulpit attached to the south side of the Chapel, one of those additions to a Gothic building which did not get much use in modern times. From there I would read the opening prayer and gospel passage before jogging back down the inside stairs and through the side door to join the procession.

The weather in New Jersey can be dicey in the early spring, but my friends in the congregation were generous in their response or at least willing to humor their Episcopal Dean. Back on went the coats and scarves as I invited them to assemble outside under the pulpit.

There, squinting up at me through some stray spring snowflakes, they offered their responses to the prayer and reading and then headed off singing into the cold air as bravely as they could without accompaniment.

I gave myself a little smile of triumph and turned from the pulpit to open the door to the stairs. It seemed to be stuck. No, the darn thing had locked itself. I rattled it a few times and futilely knocked on the thick panels. There was, of course, no one inside the Chapel to rescue me. I turned back to catch sight of the receding procession. Beginning to imagine myself stranded until they remembered where I had been left, I shouted to my associate at the rear of the procession.

Too busy with glory, laud and honor, she at first didn't hear me. "*Sue Anne, Sue Anne!*" She turned around in response to my frantic gesturing, finally realized my plight and headed back inside and up the stairs to rescue me.

Trying vainly to muster what scraps of dignity might be left but already beginning to giggle at my chagrin, we ran in flapping vestments to catch up with the riding on in majesty. We had fashioned a little mock opera of our own.

Academic processions can also have their moments, full of pomp and circumstance — suddenly drenched in a cloud burst, or, as likely in the seventies, sprayed by some wag's water pistol. Once a marshall solemnly processed the honorary degree recipients around to the wrong side of the outdoor platform where there were no steps. A less solemn procession back to the other side might have been in order, but one athletic recipient of that year high-stepped onto the platform while the others, hiking up their gowns, either scrambled or were hoisted aboard.

But back to church — where many have watched late choir members still enrobing while hurrying to catch up with his or her place in line. We have witnessed the mis-timed processions that took off without their clergy who then had to find their own straggling way into the sanctuary.

One fine Sunday afternoon, while being driven to the rededication of a restored church, I was told that the readings for the service were different from the ones I had previously been given. I spent the minutes I had in the car rapidly revising what I had planned to preach.

As the outdoor procession for that liturgy began to wend its way around the block before entering the church, I was handed the program for the service which, I wryly noted, contained yet another set of readings. Smiling in my cope and miter, this bishop was glad to have a few more minutes of solemn procession to think about whatever sermon I might preach, though I mostly spent my time being bemused by life's vagaries.

Youthful choir probationers, who will at times follow their instructions better than their elders, can help to form some interesting processions. Once, when the leading cross, torches and banner mistakenly veered off to process around the church again, they of the little cassocks and surplices stubbornly headed up into the sanctuary on their own, there, piping along, to await the others. The cross, torches and banner meanwhile headed back to follow the main choir and usher in the procession of one clergy and one lay reader, grandly led on their way by two crosses, two banners and four torches.

On another Sunday, however, it was those same probationers who followed their cross and torches in the wrong direction during one of those elaborate processions which involve a couple of trips up and down the aisles. As the probationers' procession headed back down the center aisle, they were met mid-church by the adult choir with its cross and torches, heading up. There confusion reigned for a stanza or two until, after several efforts at about face, a procession finally was formed to make its way to the sanctuary with two crosses and banners and four torches in its middle.

And all to the glory of God.

Our Families

"Will all of you witnessing these promises do all in your power to uphold these two persons in their marriage?" "We will." With and for family members, friends and members of our churches, many of us have made this promise. What do we do to fulfill it?

Today we know that families come in different shapes. With remarriage and single parents and people living together, with grandparents or aunts and uncles raising children in the absence of parents, the "traditional" family is far from being the experience of every child throughout his or her growing years. It has always been, and continues to be, an important part of our responsibility to help uphold all such families, especially when children are involved. Indeed, God repeatedly calls upon God's people to give particular care to "the widows and orphans" — we might say to all who come from "broken" families, especially when poverty and lack of opportunity to share in the benefits of society are part of their circumstances.

It is also true, however, that the great majority of children are born in marriages of a wife and husband, and I have always understood both society's and the church's primary concern with faithful relationships and a right use of sexuality to help keep these families strong and intact, especially for the sake of the children. This is not to say that other relationships are not important and valuable, but the health and well-being of society call for two-parent families wherever this is possible.

A decade or two ago it was fashionable to point out the ways so-called nuclear families could malfunction and even be stifling to the growth of children. Healthy children could grow, it was shown, in other family configurations. While no family is perfect, more experience has also shown how beneficial having both a responsible and caring mother and father can be for a child. We have seen as well the damage that can be done by the lack of such presence.

This lack is among the reasons why divorce in families with children is often such a sadness. The church is probably wise to permit divorce when marriages are irretrievably broken, especially when they truly become unhealthy for the children. And there can be new beginnings. But experience has also shown, however much we wanted to believe in "good divorces," that divorce is often hard on children. Perhaps the best gift one can give to one's children for their own marriages is the experience of being raised in a marriage trying to be a good marriage. Barbara and I have been married for thirty-six years, and we know how lucky and blessed we were and are to have come from intact and caring marriages, which was also true of their parents before them.

Not all of us can have that blessing, but we can commit to trying to share and support it wherever possible, including, too, after there has been divorce and perhaps remarriage, making the very best of the commitments involved.

What are some of the other things we can do?

Our churches are meant to be great resources for all families and marriages. I rejoice when I see churches that carefully prepare couples for marriage. This is often best done in congregations large enough to have classes where couples can also talk and share with one another. Smaller churches might join together to form such classes.

It can be very helpful to have other couples in the congregation share in the teaching and reflection. This can be an important ministry for couples in the church and strengthening for their own marriages. They can, among other things, help new marriages see that every marriage will have its flaws and problems, and that, when these emerge, it need not be the end of marriage or love. So many marriages are strengthened by living through them.

There is no wisdom in being idealistically romantic or unrealistic about marriage today. We all know the divorce statistics which predict that one out of two marriages will end in failure. We know that we live in a society where individual fulfillment and gratification have been exalted out of proportion and where a highly charged media and advertising culture has left many people feeling anxious as if lacking or unfulfilled in their sexual expression. Contraception, which can be such a help to families and marriages, has also loosened the restrictions involving pregnancy which once tended to inhibit adultery. Sadly, abortion enters into this part of the story too.

Yet, all this being true, so many women and men still join into marriage with such high hopes and sense of commitment. Many of them will make it together, and we owe to them all the support we can offer, just as we have promised.

Churches can offer parenting classes and support such ministries as Marriage Encounter. They can provide child care and assist in the education of children. It is good to bring couples together to share with and support one another, while the strength of many congregations is that they are inter-generational and can offer the mutual support of couples of different ages. Widows and widowers as well can join in. But, again, this is a ministry for all of us. Single disciples and those living in other relationships have much to offer in upholding the married and families as well. This support has certainly been there for Barbara and myself and our sons in our family experience.

Life, of course, is often busy and sometimes frenetic now. Many marriages and families experience a good deal of stress. But then life was hard for many of our parents and grandparents as well. In some ways harder. Having a good marriage and family life has always taken a lot of commitment.

In helping families with children we might share the importance of such understandings as basic as this: The other day I saw a study which showed that in families which ate at least three meals a week together (with the TV off), children were much less likely to get into trouble.

Having those three meals together tells us, of course, a lot about the family. Yet, what a good, simple piece of advice. Another is for parents to be properly involved in their children's schooling. This, too, is a distinctive marker of a strong family.

From a Christian and biblical understanding, perhaps the most important counsel we can give as a church may at first seem surprising. Don't put the family first! That is, don't turn the family itself into a selfish unity in society. Jesus warns us of that danger. Using a form of Semitic exaggeration, he even says we must be prepared to hate family relationships if they keep us from putting the concerns of the reign of God — fairness, justice, rightness, mercy, peacemaking and compassion — first.

Family members and a family who try to live in these often counter-cultural ways, and to love and serve others as themselves, will have their family values right. They will recognize that the greatest danger to a number of families is poverty, low job opportunities, poor education and health services. They will want to help strengthen the families of others. They will want to see them as our families too.

Near the end of the marriage service there is a prayer which asks that the new couple's "home may be a haven of blessing and peace." I knew homes like that when I was growing up. I believe my parents' home was one. The calling for many of us is so to live and love as to make our homes — full of noise and activity and different personalities as they may be — also full of such peace and blessing for others.

Morning Prayer

Lord God, I am up this morning as your sun rises,
   the return incredible again,
burgundy warming to gold on the horizon's hearth.

I imagine other spectacles through myriad ages,
   in different shapes, colors and speeds,
    on countless worlds of cold and fiery beauty,
and I am out of mind.

Birds herald and call me happily back.
Their trees grow green, each its own shrine.

Crowned, you burst forth, emblazoning the sky
before and beyond, reflecting all things.

And, though I think I know its dangers,
I recognize my mothers and fathers come to worship you,
for, bathed in light, I, too, am on my knees
and see beyond all times and worlds
   your shining here.

It Shall Be Opened Unto You

Let there be light, and there was light.

Be not afraid. For behold, I bring you tidings of great joy that shall come to all people. For unto you is born this day in the City of David, a savior which is Christ the Lord.

Thou shalt love the Lord thy God with all thine heart, with all thy soul and with all thy might.

Ask and it shall be given you.
Seek and ye shall find.
Knock and it shall be opened unto you.

Blessed are the pure in heart, for they shall see God.

For this thy brother was dead, and is alive again; and was lost and is found.

A city set on a hill cannot be hid.

Why seek the living among the dead? He is not here, but is risen.

With God all things are possible.

Believing that the Bible should be readily available in the language of the people, William Tyndale probably did more to shape contemporary English than any other person. More than Shakespeare. It was Tyndale, translating directly from the Greek and Hebrew, who gave Shakespeare his Bible.

It is hard now to understand how much opposition there was in the early 16th century to the translation of the Bible into English. Some of it, no doubt, came from wanting to retain the familiar and from resistance to change. It must have seemed to many that the Bible had always been in Latin. Indeed, even some who easily could have known better wanted to insist that Latin was the original language of Scripture and to deny that the Greek or Hebrew could be prior. Or, they would maintain that Latin was the inspired biblical language of the Church.

The language was important to the Church's power. After all, Thomas More and others would argue that the Church existed before the New Testament was written, and it alone could be the arbiter and interpreter of its Bible. To contend, as Tyndale and other reformers did, that anyone and any community could read and interpret Scripture on their own was subversive of the established order and the stability of institutions.

Tyndale maintained that average disciples could understand Scripture. The allegorical ways in which Scripture had been interpreted were unimportant when set beside the plain sense of the Bible. The Pope and elaborate church interpretation were not necessary. In a famous remark attributed to him, Tyndale promised that if God spared his life for the work of translation, "ere many years I will cause a boy that driveth a plough, shall know more of Scripture than thou [the Pope] knowest." The translations of the New Testament he made were "ready-to-hand" books (like our pocket books) that any person could carry.

As those New Testaments were read, others could discover that Scripture set forth two sacraments, not seven. Scripture knew not of purgatory and penance as the Church had been presenting them and upon which much of its institutional power depended. Readers could see that the rock on which Jesus said the Church was to be built was the faith which Cephas/Peter professed and not on the person of Peter himself, much less a continuing office he represented. Although to a degree more moderate than Luther in his insistence that it was faith alone which saved, Tyndale, too, found in Paul's letters, and especially in the Letter to the Romans, the key to understanding God's salvation in Christ. Good works followed the saving faith in what God had done through Christ Jesus. Works did not come first, and certainly not the kind of penitential works controlled by ecclesiastical establishment.

Even though sympathy had been growing for an English translation of the Bible (Wycliff's earlier translation from the Latin having been banned), Tyndale could find no official support for what had to be seen as a dangerous enterprise. Leaving England in 1524 or 1525, never to return, Tyndale first went to Germany and immediately set to the work of translating the New Testament, a task he likely already had begun. He had the example of Luther before him, and he used Erasmus's Greek New Testament, with its many better and earlier readings than were to be found in the Latin Vulgate Bible. Later Tyndale would also learn Hebrew and translate the Old Testament from Genesis through II Chronicles.

His first New Testaments were smuggled into England, often in bales of cloth. Their popularity is evidenced by the fact that there was money to be made from their trade and because of the risks that people were willing to take in owning them.

Cardinal Wolsey, More, the Bishop of London and others saw only danger in these English translations. In the complicated political circumstances of the time, they were able to use the specter of "Lutheranism" to convince others that these translated New Testaments were a step on the way to anarchy. They gathered together as many of the translations as they could and had them publicly burned.

Tyndale was shocked at the burning of God's holy word. But that was only the beginning of the burnings. Those who held they were doing God's work in burning English Bibles would before long find justification for burning those who did the work of translation and spread the heresies of the new thinking.

Although Tyndale found some years of relative peace and was able to publish both a revised edition of his New Testament and his translation of the first five books of the Hebrew Bible, a devious "friend" (perhaps commissioned by the Bishop of London) was able to trick him into the hands of authorities near Brussels. Although some attempt was made from England to spare him, he was strangled and burnt in October of 1536. Ironically, in but a few years King Henry, his break from the Pope now more clear, would officially sanction and welcome the Bible in the language of his people.

Much of that translation was Tyndale's. Its strength and accuracy was of such greatness that it would be taken over, almost in its entirety, into the Authorized or King James' version of 1611. Indeed, in a number of places where the later translators thought they would improve upon Tyndale, Tyndale arguably has the better of it.

Tyndale had been raised in Gloustershire and further educated in Oxford before several years in Cambridge. At that time, Latin was still the language of official affairs (of education, law and church matters), and there were a number of English dialects. Tyndale's translation of so much of the Bible into direct, common speech was critical in the forming of a common language.

He wanted the Bible to be understood. He looked for everyday words, often monosyllables. His phrases and sentences tended to be short, but with an ear for rhythm and a sense of the suppleness of the language, often making a kind of poetry.

> *I go to prepare a place for you,*
> *And if I go to prepare a place for you,*
> *I will come again and receive you unto myself,*
> *that where I am there may ye be also.*

The directness of his English is still such that he can often sound more contemporary than some of the modern translations which strive for what they may regard as a more literary effect.

A number of Tyndale's phrases have passed so fully into usage that many people may no longer know their source: *Eat, drink and be merry; the fat of the land; the powers that be; fight the good fight; signs of the times; filthy lucre; Am I my brother's keeper?; a law unto themselves; the burden and heat of the day.*

Had Tyndale been allowed to live to translate the Psalter and the prophets, there would, no doubt, be more such phrases of his.

Tyndale was also, of course, riding the tide of the future. With the spread of the printing press and changes in education, economics and the social order, the Bible in the language of the people could not long be kept out of their hands. There was a growing sense of the ability to understand for oneself, of an equality before God that the newly translated Bible itself encouraged. Tyndale would not have been subject to the kind of individualism which would later threaten an awareness of being a people together and of belonging to communities of believers, but he did not believe that a controlling establishment was a necessary intermediary between the people and God. He would likely have been appalled, too, by the development in Protestantism which led to powerful individual ministers doing the interpreting for the community. Christians living in faith together were, by faith and God's grace and Spirit, able to understand and interpret Scripture. And especially was this true when they were given not snippets — not a line or proof texts here and there — but the whole Bible, its whole drama and story, by means of which the individual parts were provided their context and understanding.

For this belief, Tyndale gave his life and gave to us so many riches of the English language and of faith.

NOTE: David Daniell is the author *William Tyndale: A Biography* (Yale University Press, 1994) and was the curator of the exhibition "Let There Be Light: William Tyndale and the Making of the English Bible" at the Huntington Library. I am indebted to his works and conversation with him for this commentary.

Between

What so distinctively is shared
could be kept *entre nous*,
sliding mid two and one;
or, say, red and a green,
linked and divided together;
or the distance from here to there,
leaving little or much as the mean,
set in ready to go with time's imprecision,
parenthesis, adverb, life's preposition,
meting out sickness and health, richer and poorer
mid longing and fears, day and/or night,
the cutting of cords, golden, umbilical
while providing the pairing
that joins and sets all apart,
ours to apportion, now and not yet,
to be held and halved, just between us.

❖　　2　　❖

Race and Grace
and
Life Together

Race and Grace

The longer I live, the more history I read, the more countries I visit, the more I am aware that most human beings prefer the company of people they regard as like themselves. That may seem a commonplace and rather innocuous observation, but it takes on more sinister aspects when one also sees that human beings tend to avoid and to discourage the company of those who are different. There are anxieties and fears of the other. Language, customs, skin color and additional features can be used to identify "others" for purposes of keeping groups at some social and often greater disadvantage.

Overtly or covertly, this distancing is regularly based in forms of prejudice regarding those who are different. There are characteristics in their makeup which, it is believed, incline them to behaviors or standards or just "ways" which seem strange. In milder forms of prejudice, these "others" may be just "not like us," but there is usually the implication that "not like us" is also not the best. In harsher kinds of prejudice, different complexions and customs are regarded as clearly inferior.

Prejudice becomes racism when a group dominant in numbers and/or in other ways (such as money, education or technology) is able to exercise its powers so as to deprive other people of equal opportunities for work, education, health care, housing, and civil rights. This can and does happen just about everywhere in the world, but it is more obvious in some societies than others.

Such racism can have subtle dimensions, encoded in practices and assumptions rather than law. The dominant group, for instance, may feel that it is willing to accept others as long as they adapt to their practices and understandings. In such cases many members of the dominant group may contend and often believe that they are uninfluenced by racism or even prejudice.

In its stronger forms racism uses the power of law and force to assert its advantages — sometimes even becoming types of apartheid. In its most abject form it countenances slavery with justifications of racial superiority. The "others" are not fully human or not human in the way the dominant group is.

It has often been maintained that prejudice is learned — that children pick it up from older family members and society. Such learning, no doubt, has considerable influence, but I do not believe it tells the whole story. I have been around little children enough to watch them begin to develop their own attitudes toward those whom they regard as different. Were we somehow able to start a society all over again, I fear that prejudice and racism would soon show themselves.

Nor do I believe that understanding the causes of prejudice and racism will change relationships, although it can be a beginning. Most dominant groups, for instance, assume that there is something about themselves (a genetic factor, an intelligence factor, an industriousness factor) which has brought them to their place of superiority. They may not articulate this assumption, but how else is their role of superiority explained? Such superiority has been particularly evident over the last centuries as those of European ancestry have easily conquered Native Americans on two continents, Australian aborigines, various African groups and others. Not only were many of these people killed, decimated by disease, enslaved or otherwise set aside, the Europeans showed themselves, at least in a number of ways, more adept at using the resources of the lands for a far more developed way of life. This in itself became justification for a takeover. If more justification was needed, one could throw in a better religion and contend to be doing this all for the good of the conquered.

Why did the Europeans win so easily? In earlier times why did people from China move so readily into southeast Asia and those peoples into Indonesia and the Philippines? Why did Bantus replace the Khosian? Why did Native Americans succumb to European diseases while little happened the other way round?

In his book *Guns, Germs and Steel*, Jared Diamond analyzes the ways in which continental shape and climate, grain size, and the availability of domesticatable animals, along with other factors, helped some cultures develop settled farming practices, larger and more complex populations, and technologies faster than others. Living in close proximity with domestic animals produced more numerous disease strains for which Europeans developed some immunities, but for which those of other continents had none.

It is a rich, fascinating and at times tragic history of many thousands of years, involving all the continents and peoples of the world. In terms of how some peoples developed better guns, germs and technologies, it helps us understand their good fortune with regard to where their societies were formed.

The Los Angeles area is the most diverse region the world has ever known. The migrations and mixings and blendings of people which are happening in other parts of the world are happening exponentially here. More than 240 identifiable ethnic groups of more than 10,000 people — with groups of hundreds of thousands and millions among them — live in this region. Just the press and mingling of people in schools and malls and work places may be of some help in new understanding and sharing, although it can also work the other way round.

Our faith teaches us that all races and peoples are of God's creation. This is the foundation for our nation's claim that "all men are created equal," although we struggle to affirm this for all men and women. Our Christian faith tells us that Jesus gave himself for everyone and that in him ("Jew or Greek, slave or free, male and female") all races, ethnicities, genders and classes are one. So do we hold before us in our mission statement the vision that we will be God's pentecost people, welcoming and sharing faith and ministry with everyone, whatever their background.

But the evidence is yet before us that for ourselves as God's people — and certainly for us as a part of our society — we require grace as well as understanding in order to live this equality out. I rejoice that there are so many parts of our diocese and so many of our congregations where one can see or at least glimpse the rainbow people of God — where we can learn more of God from our differences. Yet this also makes us more aware of how much we need a sense of our own love and acceptance — a healing of our fears and anxieties — to be able to put ourselves in others' shoes, to love our neighbors as ourselves, to respect the dignity of every human being, and to build friendships and a full and equal sharing of our humanity.

So do we learn that people of different groups face many of the same human problems, share many common concerns, and have similar hopes and aspirations. So may we promote a sense of belonging together as we face our problems and seek reconciliation and opportunities together.

Horrendous Evils

"When I get to heaven," the woman told her pastor, "I'm going to get in line to ask God why such terrible things happen in this life." "Ma'am," her pastor replied, "it's a very long line."

Holocaust and genocide, or, more personally, the lonely and painful death of a cherished friend from cancer; a father accidentally backs the car over his beloved daughter. God! Some wounds no amount of time can heal. Can they ever be overcome?

How can it be? Where is fairness? Where are justice and mercy? The questions have been asked from before Job and on. How can there be a God that is both good and mighty? Or, as process theologians and others would have it, is God good and caring but limited by the rules of creation? Even God, it is argued, cannot make square circles. God cannot make a creation without suffering and evil.

Yet what good is a God that is so limited as not to be able to prevent holocaust for his beloved people? Is God, as Woody Allen would impishly have it, an underachiever? Is this not what has caused the recession of God for many people in this secular age?

Or can the love of God yet overcome even the most horrendous of evils? Can God's sharing in the evil and suffering make some difference? Does God in some way absorb evil so that what happens to us happens to God? Can God's honoring of human suffering mean that terrible evils are finally overcome by the goodness of God?

Important and poignant as these questions are, they often seem to be caught up in debates that just go round and round. But with trenchant logic and scholarship, Marilyn Adams takes on these issues in her book *Horrendous Evils and the Goodness of God*. Writing as a practical realist and with verve and compassion, she endeavors to "kick down the dividing wall between philosophical and biblical theology." In conversation with both philosophers and theologians she creates a moving argument for the defeat of even horrendous evil by the goodness of God in the honoring of all human suffering.

Marilyn Adams is the Horace Tracy Pitken Professor of Historical Theology at Yale's Divinity School and Department of Religious Studies. She is also a priest of the Diocese of Los Angeles.

To Till and To Keep

Expecting human beings to be environmentalists is like expecting goats to be gardeners. So says the cynic. But there is a lot of evidence that the cynic is not far off the mark. Oh, we can talk a good game. When polled, the majority of people will say that environmental standards must be set very high. They also agree that we should spare little cost in caring for the environment.

Once again, talk is cheap. Special interests quickly enter into the picture. It is, we are told, a matter of jobs or profit margins. Or it is the needs of the consumer driven economy or of military security. Or all of the above, meaning that environmental concerns must come in a distant second. Just as often the special interest is you or me. If there are sacrifices of some kind that need to be made for the common good, someone else will need to go first.

It is alarming to watch the generation that was taught at least something about the environment (and sometimes came home and lectured their parents about it), now falling for the auto makers' bamboozles and choosing vehicles with little care for conservation and the environment. So much for education! Here we were given a decade of relative economic prosperity to do something about our over-consumption of fossil fuels, and instead we have blithely increased them our use of them.

Maybe a good deal of our problem is, in fact, the result of a kind of thoughtlessness. I sometimes wonder what urban and suburban people imagine when they pick up those cellophane wrapped packages of chopped meat in the refrigerated display. Or even the nicely manufactured little round cereal O's. Where could these have come from? Or where does water come from? The faucet. Electricity? The wall. And then where do things go? Flush and it's gone. Engine oil or paint goes down the drain. They disappear.

The only cost we tend to reckon with is what it cost us in dollars and cents. And there are even times when tomorrow will have to care of that. The watchword of more than one generation becomes "whatever."

No doubt self-centeredness and our "affluenza" are also part of the story. Human anxiety breeds a fear that we are not getting our share and that others are getting more. Advertising cleverly fuels this, and many people find themselves trapped in the mall. What we so greatly need is a new vision — a different perspective on ourselves and our relationship with one another and with nature.

Adam is placed in the garden both "to till it and keep it" (Genesis 2:15). This is no romantic picture. The earth must be used to grow food and to help provide other of life's necessities. But there are also ways to use it without using it up. There are ways to use nature so it can be reused — so that it can be kept. One image we could hold up before ourselves is that of the sailor using the wind. Picture it — using but not using up with plenty to share. Not everything in life is like that, but maybe more can be as anxiety's greed eases and the common good strengthens. There are ways of making electricity without using up.

Another image we might reflect on is going to the beach. If we would let it happen, access to the beaches might be pretty much closed off. If it became only a right of owners "to do what I want with my own," the good beaches would be walled off by hotels, condominiums and estates. But we have said *no*. Or better we have said *yes*. At least many beaches and their waters should be open to everyone. Maybe we could begin to think similarly of clean water and air and sanitation. None of us can take that from each other. Perhaps one day we can extend such understanding and generosity to health care and to education.

We are coming to the end of an incredible century. Those living in 1899 could not have believed it. They could not have believed the scientific and technological marvels by means of which we now communicate, process information, travel and extend the human life span. Nor could they have believed the wars and genocide. They would have been amazed of what we are capable of making, having and knowing, while human empathy, kindness and generosity continue to be so fragile. So many goods with little or no growth in sharing the common good.

"The stewardship of all creation in the next century" is the theme for our forthcoming diocesan convention. We intend that the issues and the vision we hold up there will be ours in the months and years to come. In doing so we will be thinking about the whole of our lives: the stewardship of our gifts and talents, of our money, of our relationships with one another and with the environment. These concerns and opportunities for change stand out among the most important spiritual challenges we together face! A changed people and culture are needed. Stay tuned!

Living Wage

This op-ed article (co-authored with Rabbi Leonard Beerman and Methodist Bishop Roy Sano) was originally published in the Los Angeles Times *in December of 1996, and appeared in* The New York Times *in February of 1997. It was the opening shot in a campaign that led to thousands of workers being included in "living wage" ordinances and other wage agreements in the Los Angeles area. The campaign continues. For more on the issues and efforts see* The Living Wage: Building a Fair Economy *by Robert Pollin and Stephanie Luce (The New Press. 1998).*

"You shall not withhold the wages of the poor and needy laborer." Those words, written centuries ago in Deuteronomy, are being taken to heart here as the Los Angeles City Council considers a "living wage" ordinance.

The living wage being discussed is enough to bring a family of four up to the federal poverty level — $7.50 and hour plus health coverage and other benefits or $9.50 an hour without those benefits. The ordinance would apply to those companies holding service contracts with or receiving subsidies from the city.

Some have attacked the ordinance as unrealistic and unaffordable, but two recent studies show that it can be implemented with little impact on the city budget, no employment loss and no loss of city services. This is good news. But as a moral people we need to examine values, not only costs.

How much do we value the people who work in our city? What are their lives worth? Let's make it personal. Let's think about a father of two who makes his living as a janitor cleaning a Los Angeles landmark, the Central Library. His employer is the company that holds the maintenance contract.

The janitor now works six days a week and makes $4.75 an hour, taking home approximately $700 a month in a county where the average monthly rent for a two-bedroom apartment is $855. His wife has diabetes, but his job does not have medical benefits. That is also why he did not seek medical attention when he hurt his back a few month ago. It's everything he can do to pay the $115 monthly bill for the family's medications.

In another case, Elvira (not her real name) works in a meat-packing plant that received a low-interest $4.6-million loan through the city to move to Los Angeles. She supports herself and her 5-year-old daughter on $4.75 an hour, or $9,880. The plant is cold, but she is expected to pay for jackets and gloves out of her earnings.

City contracts are certainly sufficiently lucrative to pay a living wage. The company that contracts to clean the Central Library nets an estimated annual profit of more than 36 percent (based on an analysis of their contract and interviews with knowledgeable people in the offices of the city's chief legislative analyst and General Services Department).

We have the right and responsibility to see that such employees are paid enough to support themselves and their families in basic dignity. We have a right and a responsibility to say to businesses: If you want to benefit from our tax dollars, then we can require that all who do the labor are paid at least a living wage.

A fair and living wage not only makes ethical sense, it also makes good economic sense. People who can feed and care for their families and provide for their medical care are no longer dependent on the social services that taxpayers must otherwise provide. Indeed, when we think about it, why should we allow companies that benefit from our tax dollars to pay their workers less than a living wage and then leave the rest of us to pay for health care and food stamps?

A healthy society — less poverty, less crime, more people with a stake in the community — is what will most help businesses in Los Angeles. By not withholding the wages of the poor and needy laborer, we are all better off as a people.

Work

In April of 1999 a national consultation on Work Economics and Theology was held at the Cathedral Center of St. Paul in Los Angeles. This led to the publication of Let Justice Roll Down: American Workers at the New Millennium *and a video with the same name that included footage of various aspects of the living wage campaign from scenes with workers at the Los Angeles International Airport and at several Beverly Hills hotels. The following essay was a contribution to the consultation.*

"By the sweat of your face you shall eat bread," God tells Adam, just before he is expelled from the Garden (Genesis 3:19). We may think it would be nice to dwell in the Garden of Eden, but if human beings were only to live in some paradise, life would be a lot less interesting. Much that is worthwhile requires some form of labor and effort.

Viewed historically, most of the work of humanity has been directly involved with providing the necessities of life — especially enough food: gathering it, growing it, hunting it, preparing it. There could be some division of labor based on age and gender, though all but the littlest and weakest members of society had work to do, if not with providing food, then with other necessities.

Although there have always been times of famine and drought and competition for food, and always the fear that the weakest would be left out (hence the biblical admonitions about care in the community for the children and widows), there were also times of satisfaction. Humans could be grateful for the fruits of their labor, feel a harmony with the world and nature, and find pleasure in providing for dependents and others in the community. There was a sense of participation and even vocation, and, in this way, a genuinely human and spiritual dimension to work.

As settled communities found means to grow enough food so that all members were not directly involved in its production, society began to grow more complex. Some members could take up various crafts. There could be artisans and managers, teachers and philosophers, along with more opportunity for the trade of the products of labor. Certain forms of hierarchy developed and with them new measures of inequality and coerciveness.

One could still look, however, for the basic dimensions of the significance of labor: an opportunity to provide livelihood for self and any dependents, and a way of participating in the life of the community. At best there came with this work a sense of satisfaction and of contributing to the welfare — even the betterment of others' lives. As societies developed, there was more opportunity for collaboration and cooperative effort. Hard work was tolerable as long as one could find it meaningful.

The greatest changes in the character and understanding of work came with the industrial revolution. Technological development meant less need for human muscle and more need for at least certain kinds of education and training. Fewer people were required actually to grow and produce the food, but pools of labor were needed to manufacture a greater number of goods and services. Capital became important as the way to provide equipment, machinery and further technology.

Complexity grew apace along with further inequalities. Many workers tended to be part of a chain of manufacturing, farther away from the final product and any direct benefits of their labor. Members of large chains were more anonymous in their labor, more readily replaced. The holders of capital began to see pools of laboring people as a resource which could be manipulated to produce greater return on capital. In response, workers sometimes banded together into unions to contract for their labor, and there were periods of highly adversarial relationships.

These summary observations are, of course, but a thin plot line in an immensely complicated story. The story tells of much human achievement along with loss and degradation. Chapters of adversarial relationships are interspersed with those of greater rewards and appreciation of labor, and learning the values of cooperation and working together. Industrial and technical progress has moved more rapidly in some parts of society and of the world than in others. In many areas it has now moved on to the information and Internet age with an even greater valuing of information processing, education, international trade and resourcing, together with the growing role of multinational corporations.

In all this one can still ask, however, what is the significance of work? In personal terms, many people would probably continue to respond that they want their work to enable them to provide a decent livelihood for themselves and any dependents, and a way of participating in the life and benefits of the community. They would hope for an opportunity to use their skills and talents, to develop them and to learn, and so gain a sense of competence and satisfaction in their labor and of their contribution to the welfare and even the betterment of others' lives. Thus, they could find a vocation and a spiritual dimension to their work, factors which may seem more obviously fulfilled in some occupations than others (nursing, teaching and so forth) but may be found in almost any labor if one wishes so to regard it. One thinks of Brother Lawrence with his broom sweeping to the glory of God and George Herbert's "What I do in anything, to do it as for thee."

This, however, is to put the best face on the opportunities for work in our society, for there are also many ongoing problems and difficulties. Here are just two areas in which questions may be raised. What are the effects on the sense of the value and purpose of labor when there is great wealth and wage disparity? The president of one corporation is paid many millions of dollars. The strawberry pickers who work for the corporation earn less than ten thousand dollars annually. This is not an unusual situation, especially in the United States where top executives are often paid hundreds of times more than non-supervisory employees. To what degree should a company be responsible to its workers as well as its stockholders and executives?

Workers in certain areas of society which once had more of a service orientation (for example, helping to manage other people's money, assisting people and business in legal matters, assisting financial markets and relationships) now in many cases have a powerful leverage on financial resources and rewards. Public high school teachers, many of them with considerable education and whose work is critical to the future of the community, are among society's lower paid workers. Yet the work of financial managers may also be regarded as beneficial to society. In what measures? We speak of open markets setting wages and salaries, but what forces work to keep those markets from being too open? Why, in a time of great wealth production in the United States, does eighty percent of the population receive a smaller share of the nation's total income than it did twenty years ago? In Los Angeles County, more than one-third of workers make under $15,000; eighty-eight percent of those without health insurance are workers or their dependents.

Then what of those who are without work or whose only work does not produce a wage enabling them to have access to vital services such as health care and useful education? In a society which seems largely to value people only if they work or have other financial means (otherwise they have at best limited access to decent food, shelter, safety and health care in their communities), what responsibility do we collectively have to provide decent work and wages for each other? How might this benefit the whole of society?

In his book *When Work Disappears: The World of the New Urban Poor,* William Julius Wilson shows how the loss of work for certain classes and groups in our society has led to a devastating cycle of poverty, family breakdown and blighted neighborhoods. He holds out hope, however, for a change in these conditions and a benefit for the whole of society if more opportunities for decent wage work can be created.

In *The Human Enterprise: a Christian Perspective on Work*, Richard Gillett maintains that "The question of work may be the critical global social issue... The other critical social issues — adequate housing, hunger and massive migratory movements of people, the incredible burden upon society of a global arms race, the degenerating urban centers of the world, the basic human need to feel productive and creative — would become much less critical if the core issue of work could be effectively addressed." Similarly, Pope John Paul, in his 1981 encyclical *On Human Work*, held that "Human work is a key, probably the essential key to the whole social question."

The issues are complex, but one could become more optimistic about our society if through our churches and in other ways we could build a majoritarian moral, political and economic consensus which recognizes that it is to everyone's benefit to provide work with a living wage and health benefits for all. When the poor are able to become full participants in the economy, the whole of life becomes larger. We could then more effectively share these benefits with others in our world.

Energy

Energy comes in many forms: physical, mental and spiritual. Life works best when they are working together. The Greek root word means work, act, deed. Energy is what does this work. Throughout much of history, human muscles supplied the energy for hunting, farming, fishing, building, shaping and moving things. Horses, oxen and other animals were then harnessed to help, and, in the flowering of pre-industrial technology, ingenuity made use of the wheel and lever, water and wind power to augment human efforts. The saga of the building of the transcontinental railroad is a story of the meeting of the pre-industrial and industrial worlds. Prodigious use of human muscle was assisted by horses and early technology to enable the steam engine to link America together.

Steam, followed by gasoline engines and the development of electrical power, dramatically changed the way most people lived. The continent could be crossed in a week instead of the months that earlier journeys took. Telegraphic messages were sent instantly. Then lights, automobiles, tractors, central heating, powered machinery, radio, vacuum cleaners, television, jet airplanes, the Internet and all manner of other technology assumed many human burdens and speeded up the pace of life.

All this development has brought enormous benefits and, in many societies, helped to make life more egalitarian by distributing a number of these benefits to the labor force and the poorer classes of people. At the same time, however, economic forces have been at work that have put the greatest wealth from natural sources of energy in the control of a relatively small portion of the population. Not least in the United States, the tendency has been to place non-renewable energy resources (coal, oil, natural gas), along with other goods such as the airwaves, into private hands and trust that competitive market forces will lead to the best development for the great majority. This entrustment has been less true with waterpower (and such other common goods as roads to travel on, basic education, beach access, water and sanitation), although there is always advocacy for more privatization and commercial ownership. Generally speaking, where money is to be made, the argument is also made that commercialization will bring the greatest overall benefits. For the most part, government (asked to be the will of the people, but also historically heavily influenced by monied interests) has supported commercialization. As nonrenewable energy sources come into shorter supply, and because electricity is now so necessary for modern life, there may in the future be more debate about the best ways to own, develop and share what can be seen as common or community goods and resources.

It is possible, too, that the usage of nuclear energy will be revisited in the United States. The dangers of nuclear energy, in my opinion, have been exaggerated when compared to the dangers of pollution from fossil fuels, although the very difficult matter of nuclear waste disposal still needs intelligent and expensive work. Good common planning and scientific effort need also to be put into the development of solar, wind and other renewable energy sources, although they may never be more than additions to the total supply of energy.

Conservation and energy efficiency (both in production and usage) are also controversial but necessary if we are to be good stewards of the creation we have been given. They, too, call upon our intelligence and caring — upon our mental and spiritual energies. In the past, because of the forces of commercialization and the relative cheapness of electricity, natural gas and gasoline, the tendency has been to promote more and more usage and to view these as almost unlimited resources. One result has been for the United States, with five percent of the world's population, to become user of nearly thirty percent of the world's energy resources. Twenty percent of the world's population, while using eighty percent of the resources, sometimes urges developing countries to be more conservative and environmentally cautious in their energy development. Unless fuel efficiency and thoughtful and caring conservation become an integral part of energy usage in the United States, it is hard to see how we can be viewed as a responsible society in this regard.

We probably become most aware of our personal physical, mental and spiritual energies when they are in short supply. One of the downsides of the energy and technological revolutions is that fewer than twenty-five percent of U.S. adults get enough exercise to feel vital and energized. The resultant proclivity to overweight adds to the problem.

In another irony, the anxieties of daily life, impelled by the "hurry worry" of the many options and rapid changes of informational and technological development and the demands for multi-tasking, can leave people feeling stressed out by the pace that oil and electrical energy fuels. Wealth, which essentially gives the power to pay for other people's talents, time and effort, can be stressfully sought to expand one's options and in the hope of eventually being able to lead a more leisurely life.

Pills and other short-cut strategies are attempted to restore vigor for living. Most of us know, however, that there are no substitutes for a more thoughtful pace and style of life. Compared to our forebears, I can save a lot of time by flying coast-to-coast in five hours, but what I most need is the wisdom to use the time saved with more vitality and enthusiasm for daily living.

Our richest resource for health and vitality is the spiritual energy that helps to guide the ways we live and the choices we make. Since our insecurities make us anxious about our place in life, and fearful that others may be getting more than we are, only knowing that we are already understood, forgiven and valued can calm us and bring a greater peace.

That peace (found in prayer, reflection and appreciation, in taking the time for relationships and empathy) is not mere tranquility but a storehouse of energy for living in peace and fairness with others. In this it differs from the self-help spiritualities that focus mostly on the self. An enlarging spirituality empowers the capacity for taking one's neighbor into account, making space for them in life, and seeking to understand and love them. It means being ready with great enthusiasm and enjoyment to use without using up, to conserve and share the commonwealth of the resources of life so that there can be enough for all.

Scripture relates that power (in Greek the *dunamis*, from which comes our word dynamo) of Jesus' ministry was able to overcome the powers of evil spirits and forces. This power of love enabled him to do works of healing and to change the lives of Zacchaeus, Bartimaeus, Mary Magdalene and his disciples. "Greater works," Jesus said to his disciples, "will you do," for the source of this energy is the love of God that encourages us to love and be generous with one another.

This love is the greatest energy source of all. Divine love — ever giving and ever living, as symbolized in the flame of the burning bush, is inexhaustible. In Paul's words, only "love never ends." Ultimately only such love could let be and sustain all the energy of creation that that we have been given to appreciate. This is the love that, in the culmination of Dante's great vision, "moves the sun and all other stars" and, as we respond to it, may energize human hearts as well.

The Invisible Hand

First published in the Los Angeles Times *and then in other newspapers at the height of the electricity crisis in California, this essay in irony created a fair amount of correspondence. Its point was not to deny an important place for free markets where there is genuine competition, but to ask people to think about how unquestioning trust in "the invisible hand" could become blind faith, masking, among other problems, the power of strongly positioned corporations to buy influence through campaign contributions, to operate secretively and always to try to maximize and sometimes manipulate profits. Such faith can also become an excuse for not using intelligent planning skills and wisdom with respect to responsibilities, one for another, in regard to life's basic needs.*

More than 200 years ago, Adam Smith, the Scottish philosopher and founder of economic theory, fashioned the image of the "invisible hand" to explain how myriad individual choices within a free enterprise system could lead to maximum production. While Smith held that the competitive system must be embedded in appropriate legal and institutional frameworks and valued the roles of government and taxation, the popular idea later took on a life of its own, suggesting that there were few if any areas of human endeavor in which the hand should not profitably have free reign.

The theory has even developed mystical and quasi-religious undertones. A deistic god sets the proper principles of the world's economy in motion and now needs to do little else than observe the invisible handiwork. A natural theology provides an economic and political creed: This is the way things are and are meant to be. Social Darwinism buttresses the faith, at least as far as markets, if not people, are concerned: Only the most competitive and efficient survive. Utilitarianism joins the chorus, with the praise that this brings the greatest good to the greatest number of people.

Ideologies and religions need their theologians. Arguments in favor of free competition and the most unregulated possible markets point out the failures of communism and state-sponsored socialism. Capitalism, in contrast, has proved to be universally successful. Indeed, almost all government is evil to the extend that it does not keep hands off the hand. Markets based on self-interest, and that take into account and even sanction natural human greed, are the only way to sort out economies and people.

But faith in an invisible hand becomes a form of piety. Competing evidence can be explained away. Questions may well be treated as heresy. This is serious business. On the lips of eloquent spokesmen, the gospel becomes deeply personal and moving, not least in witness to the ways individual initiative is everywhere rewarded.

Certain activities, such as policing, sewage disposal, garbage collecting and firefighting, may for now need to be managed by the community. Even here, however, other possibilities could be considered, and the wealthy, who so often lead the way in worship of the hand, are already developing markets of their own in some of these areas.

Meanwhile, not only is higher education best left to the invisible hand, but private schools and vouchers may well be the wave of the future, from preschool through high school. Transportation can be given over to the hand, as happened with Amtrak and the railroads in Britain. Deregulation of the airlines has been a blessing. Eventually, all public transportation will likely be seen as a failed social experiment. Certainly the free hand will be terrific for electricity, once supply and demand are allowed to kick in fully and the environmentalists are put in their place. Speaking of which, the hand will eventually take care of the environment, too.

One of the wonderful things about faith in the hand is that it absolves humans of the responsibility of doing the work of hard thinking and cooperative planning. If the public sector isn't doing things well, just turn them over to the hand. One must believe that resultant tax cuts will benefit everyone. There is no need to develop common goods with respect to the necessities of life because competition will provide them at the proper price. Look at what this has done for health care in the United States. Water, too, might one day be metered out in a similar manner.

Since everything works out for the best without common efforts, untrammeled free enterprise, even if it must sometimes administer pain, is the most compassionate way to do business. Such a faith can get rid of the very idea of welfare. It also can be used to encourage the taking up of collections to help elect politicians who will end any governmental interference with the work of the hand. All praise to the hand.

Liberty and Government

The purpose of government, many today would say, is to allow persons the freedom to choose a lifestyle giving maximum expression to their uniqueness and individuality. But can such an understanding of government and of individual liberty sustain the political community and civic engagement needed for the self-government upon which such liberty depends? It may seem a kind of paradox: Can a people retain and exercise personal liberties without some willingness to sacrifice private desires for public ends?

Many of the founders of this country and a number of their successors believed that self-government depended on a virtuous and civic-minded citizenry and that it was part of the task of government to encourage the kind of society which would support such civic-mindedness and its virtues.

Thomas Jefferson feared the development of a mercantile economy because of his concern that people who were not self-employed and who were without some stake in ownership of their labor would not make good citizens. Others would later worry about the development of industrial, wage-based economy for the same reason. One of the reasons for questioning the value of welfare was the concern that it would undermine the ability of recipients to participate in the responsibilities of citizenship. For similar cause, some worried that too much wealth disparity would undermine the sense of common purpose and participation necessary for genuine democracy.

In subsequent generations, political and societal leaders were concerned that big business and big financial interests could erode a sense of belonging and responsibility in the average citizen. One response, especially approved by Teddy Roosevelt, was to espouse the development of equally powerful governmental institutions to counter and regulate such bigness in business, while others feared that bigness of government could also make the citizenry feel less involved and less in charge of its destiny.

Earlier in this century there was considerable opposition to the development of large chain stores. The opposition was, however, not based primarily on economic grounds. One could see that these stores brought lower prices and larger corporate profits, at least for a time. Rather was the concern over preserving the quality of life and the values that smaller shops and local ownership brought to the community. As the people acting together, government, it was held, should help decide whether or to what extent the development of the large stores should take place. In some of our smaller communities, the debate has recently resurfaced.

In his book *Democracy's Discontent: America in Search of a Public Philosophy*, Michael Sandel describes how the economically based arguments, along with arguments in support of the rights of individuals and corporate interests to make their own unencumbered choices, won out. Over the years Roosevelt's New Deal, influenced by forms of Keynesian economics, came to accept the understanding that what would most benefit people and, therefore, what should be the main work of government, was the promotion of the economy with a particular emphasis on personal consumption. "The major part of the activity of all of us," Harold Ickes contended, "is that of consuming. It is as consumers that we all have a common interest, regardless of what productive work we may be engaged in... We work in order that we may consume." (Sandel, p. 267).

Consumer welfare and rights became central to a broader movement, stressing the civil rights of individuals and groups and the economic rights of individuals and corporate and business interests to do what they deemed best with their own. In this development there were different emphases, along with potential as well as actual conflicts. Without the right of wage laborers to organize and to withhold their labor, their ability to have some control over their own work and wages could be severely limited. Yet their rights came up against the rights of ownership to determine work conditions and pay scales.

The civil rights movement itself could, however, be cited as an example of a more communal effort, often using governmental means to forbid discrimination, to affect the moral character of our society and relationships within it. It was a movement that often had bi-racial, multi-religious and even bi-partisan and nationwide support. Affirmative Action was a follow-up effort to try to overcome some of the effects of discrimination, while it, in turn, has proved to have its complications and even paradoxes as more and more the language of rights has prevailed in the courts, in legislatures and in political debate. The voice of a more communal conservatism was replaced by a new conservatism based largely on neo-liberal and often libertarian arguments for economic and private property rights. A number of conservatives were also strongly supportive of the rights of corporations.

Meanwhile, the older liberals, having placed their bets on the advantages of growing consumption for everyone and on the defense of individual and certain group rights, had few other ways of thinking about the good of society. Despite some different emphases, both sides now had, in effect, agreed that rights were trumps and that any other matters involving the common good, shared values and virtues, morality and religion were not to be of public concern. As long as decisions regarding moral and ethical issues did not impinge directly on the lives of others, these were matters of private choice. The matters could be argued on the peripheries but were not governmental issues. The role of government was to protect rights, and not in any other way to seek to promote understandings about values and the public good. Individuals were to determine what was good for themselves. Government should be neutral.

Advantages to this public philosophy can certainly be pointed to — perhaps most prominently the protection of minority rights and ways of life from majoritarian control. Indeed, a number of voices of so-called liberal religion seem at times to have made this the centerpiece of their moral agenda.

But, when rights are trumps over efforts to discuss and perhaps establish some common goods, virtues and responsibilities, there are disadvantages for society as well. The care of the environment is one example. Despite considerable lip-service (when polled more than eighty percent of voters in the United States say that "environmental standards cannot be too high" and that improvement must be made "regardless of cost") it is often hard to establish the common good over the economic and private property rights of those opposed to significant measures of their regulation.

Among the ironies of contemporary life is a growing sense of powerlessness just at a time when individual rights seem most guaranteed. To many these rights often seem puny when up against massive market, media and other economic forces, and the amounts of money used to purchase access to and to influence elected officials. Along with this frustration has come a diminished sense that any attempts to exercise common control through government could have much value. Because government is also seen as a danger to the exercise of free rights, there are frequent calls for the limitation of government and a marked withdrawal from participation in democratic processes. A growing discontent and frustration are fed by uncertainties over how to respond. The propensity to want government and even political debate to be neutral in matters of the public good makes it difficult to know how and if to hold the discussion.

The diminishing of the habits of good citizenship, the sense of powerlessness and the withdrawal from democratic processes fuel the worry that the very basis for the self-government which is necessary to sustain individual liberties could be eroding. One can foresee forms of oligarchy and plutocracy, and then even tyranny which could eventually win out over a people unable to govern themselves.

In what measure should Christians be concerned with these questions and issues? As St. Paul might say, much in every way.

For all who find democracy to be the better form of government to help in the valuing of the worth and dignity of every human being and for the practice of Christian faith, there are strong reasons to care for cooperative attitudes and virtues which will nourish and support self-government.

Christians may share in the concern that the understanding of liberty which primarily views each individual as an unencumbered self seeking one's own achievement and development does not adequately take into account our relationships and responsibilities for one another and may, among other things, underlie the challenge to family life and the frequency of divorce and absentee parents in our society. Although some conservative Christians seem almost exclusively focused on morality dealing with sexuality issues, and at times to be unquestionably allied with libertarian economic politics, along with other Christians they may want to raise the question as to whether the economics of the growth of private consumption should be king and queen of governmental policy in lieu of a greater care for common goods, and whether individual rights should always be prior to policies encouraging civic responsibility and public virtues and duty. As challenging and complex as they often are, religious and moral questions about the character of society and our responsibilities for one another, could, rather than being bracketed by a government seeking neutrality and therefore always taking the side of individual rights, have a better place in public discussion and debate. Christians who are by their faith called not to be centered on the consuming self but to have care for others and the common good, should have much to contribute to the stock of societal strengths.

Avoiding the humiliation of others due to the lack of their most basic needs, helping to provide work for all able persons, for their educational opportunities and medical care, dealing with crime, and the common concern for adequate gun control, and the heavy doses of violence on television, attention to the potential dangers of growing disparities in wealth and control of capital power, the place of public investment for things needed by all in relation to private consumption, caring for the most destitute: these ought to be among the moral societal goals even of a people not always agreeing on how best to achieve them. Perhaps smaller, more responsible and local forms of government can help. Even with the possible loss of price savings and corporate earnings, similar issues might be raised about the size of corporations and business conglomerates. It is, after all, our lives together and our governance which is at stake.

Such basic questions certainly pose their difficulties and dangers. Some liberal and libertarians on both sides of the political fence will continue to say, "That's none of your business, and certainly it is not the business of our governance." But — in the face of massive forces at work in our society and, given the tendencies toward disillusion, discontent with and withdrawal from government — they may have become unavoidable issues for all who would support the liberties of self-government.

Almighty Buck

The recent actions or threats of several dioceses to withhold or sharply curtail their fair share giving to the Foreign and Domestic Missionary Society is not a new story in the Episcopal Church. One remembers similar action by dioceses angry over the General Convention Special Program which was designed to strengthen black ministries and empowerment during the time when John Hines was Presiding Bishop. On other occasions parishes have mounted like threats against giving through their dioceses as have individuals to their congregations.

In the largely libertarian society in which we live it is not hard to be sympathetic. Relatively few people even want to pay taxes for the common good unless it is pretty clearly their good. I love the irritated response of some of our compatriots to the savings-and-loan fiasco of several years ago: "The taxpayers shouldn't have to pay for this. The government should."

Most of us have causes about which we have felt or feel passionately. They range or have ranged from the Vietnam War, to disinvestment in South Africa, to gun safety control, from support for or being against certain gay and lesbian ministries, to abortion issues, from baptismal regeneration and the wearing of particular vestments, to the ordination of women, to Affirmative Action, to international debt, to divorce when children are involved, to land mines. We haven't wanted or don't want to give our support to a government or organization or church which is not on the right side of the issues. We grow frustrated because we cannot change things. At least we'd like to withhold that portion of our support which we think may go to help that with which we do not agree.

If we do act on our convictions, the usual strategy is to say that it is a matter of conscience. If it is a church matter, it then also becomes important to make it a matter of theology — not infrequently based in scriptural interpretation. The history of American Protestantism is, as we know, littered with the results of such controversies which escalated into division and separate denominations.

There is, however, another aspect to these controversies which may be even more dangerous to the Christian witness. It is the role of money itself.

When I was a boy growing up in our church, I was bothered by the way the collection was brought forth in solemn procession, then lifted up on high before the money was placed on the altar. It seemed to me we were worshipping money. The priest explained, however, that the money was being offered to God and that we were really giving it up so that it could be consecrated to use for the church and for others. I think I was fairly well convinced, although I was also old enough to know that it might not be quite that easy and that money was still powerful stuff.

Then I also heard stories about members of the parish who were threatening to withdraw their pledge if something wasn't done the way they approved. In one case it had to do with what a priest had said in a sermon — in another about a stained glass window. Later it concerned changes in the Prayer Book. At one point my staunchly Republican father, who was at the time a member of the vestry, told me about a man who had withdrawn his rather substantial pledge because he thought the church had become wrongly involved in some issue. The man, my father told me, had said that, "if the vestry won't listen to me, then maybe they'll have to listen to the power of the almighty buck."

"You cannot worship God and mammon." Jesus' disciples are not to worship God and money. Most of us, while still trying to perform a delicate balancing act, understand this largely as an issue of not being too addicted to affluence and material things. But mammon and money are, of course, more subtle than that. Money — "my money," "our money" — is even more about power, the desire to command resources, to overcome our anxieties, to have what others have, to buy others' labor, to gain social and political influence, to be in control, to show others. Here is the real spiritual issue.

Often we wish to hide the issue from ourselves. This is among the reasons we can often be so anxious, grudging and secretive and why we have buried guilt feelings about money in our society and even in our congregations and dioceses. We are dealing in power, machismo, and control and they call forth our worship — even after the money is placed on the altar.

We want to insist otherwise. We want to say it is really a matter of conscience. To some degree that may well be. But it is regularly also about something else. It is about money's control and power. We may have a hard time seeing that when we are involved. But just ask the outside observers. They can tell in a minute what's really going on. And that becomes our witness to the world.

When I was in Ghana recently, celebrating one of the companion relationships of our diocese, I was offering the Eucharist with the disciples in the cathedral in Accra. When it came time for the offertory, several of the younger people formed a band with some great songs and rhythm. There was then none of this sitting in the pews with solemn faces as the plates were passed. Instead, beginning from the rear of the church, humming and sometimes dancing and signing, waving handkerchiefs and smiling to friends, the congregation came forward to give its gifts.

I imagine there were people there that Sunday who did not like some cathedral policy or an action on the part of the diocese, but at least in that worship such matters did not seem to be on their minds. I'm sure that this time of giving in thanksgiving was good for stewardship, but what I saw beneath that was something far more important and joyful — a victory of God over mammon and the almighty buck.

Common Sense and Campaign Finance Reform

'No one in the history of American politics has ever won or lost a campaign on the subject of campaign finance reform." So claims Senator Mitch McConnell, chairman of the Republicans' Campaign Committee, counting as he does so on public indifference. Even after the revelations regarding the huge amounts spent in the last election and the chicanery of members of both political parties, it is said that most Americans are largely apathetic.

I hear something very different. I hear a deep and pervasive cynicism. I hear it among young and old, black, brown and white, in clubs and in barrios, from those who vote and those who do not, Republicans and Democrats. The political and governmental process is the subject of jokes, not infrequently accompanied by sneers. One wonders how many of those in public office really understand that kind of apathy and its corrosive power. No individual campaigns may be being won or lost, but trust in government is losing badly. In private conversations one discovers how the cynicism affects the politicians themselves.

No doubt a number of citizens give to campaigns to make their views known, but that is not where most the big money is. That money is about obtaining access to elected officials. Such access is troubling enough to many individual voters. If they want to make their voice known at all, they are told they will have to give to various lobbying groups.

But of course it is more than access. It is access plus for the big givers. it is being heard and well heard in exchange for money, and it is about the donation for the next campaign. On this score you don't even fool some of the people some of the time. It is the reason for the sneering when a politician claims not to be influenced by the donations.

People I know also shake their heads when they gain some sense of the time and effort politicians now devote to fund raising. Is there so little to good, informed governance that our representatives can spend hundreds of hours and untold energy on the phone or at parties, or in private meetings and traveling about raising these bucks? Nor can the majority of politicians help but be influenced just by the amount of time they spend around people of means and with financial clout.

One political party would have us believe that the situation could in part be rectified if labor unions had to poll their members before contributing or were only allowed to give money which had been donated for a particular purpose. Not a bad idea. But it just adds to the cynicism when such restrictions are advocated for the unions and not for corporations. It may be true that I can invest my money where I want to, but why should I be obliged to opt out of mutual funds and shop around just to find corporations which won't use my money to buy influence I do not want? Nor do I have any choice where my pension fund invests.

We would not, of course, be in these circumstances unless a number of individuals and groups believed they benefited from the system or at least felt forced to comply. Labor unions, corporations, various business associations, real estate groups, tobacco companies, the N.R.A., pro-life, and pro-choice. Few of us have any idea how many such groups or organizations there are. For many of them, money and money-lobbying are the ways things get done and how they get their ways.

Mitch McConnell, with some help from the Supreme Court, says it is a matter of free speech. But of course, it isn't free at all. It is very expensive. Hence all the jokes and cynicism, and the feeling on the part of many others that their speech and vote don't count for much.

One might be tempted to give up if the concerns were not so troubling and escalating, and if one did not know that there were other democratic countries and even some of our states which have common-sense practices and laws that far more fairly control what has been allowed, especially in our federal elections, to grow so out of control. It is a time for common-sense efforts in a country which was begun by a revolution based on common-sense appeals to fair and equal representation.

A Theology of Evolution

' Any thoughts we may have about God after the life and work of Charles Darwin (1809-1882) can hardly remain the same as before."

With these words John F. Haught, professor of theology at Georgetown University and director of the Georgetown Center for the Study of Sciences and Religion, introduces his book, *God After Darwin: A Theology of Evolution.* In conversation and debate with the anti-theistic evolutionary materialists (e.g. Richard Dawkins, Daniel Dennett), fundamentalist and "conservative thinkers who deny or minimize revolutionary understandings, liberals who may too glibly say they accept evolutionary theory without thinking through its implications, and those who would keep religion and scientific thought in separate spheres," Haught presents a theology of evolution informed by the broadly accepted claims of modern Darwinian theory.

Natural theology (especially one that leaves out the roles of novelty and oddity), any theological hierarchy that places humankind above the rest of creation, the problems of evil, the basis of morality, creation and eschatology are all issues that must be rethought. Beliefs or theories about intelligent design need to be profoundly re-examined in the light of the awareness that the processes of natural selection over eons of time can explain what once was understood (e.g. the development of the eye, the brain) to be the product of "skyhooks."

Nor, we may add, are these matters just for academic theologians. Evolutionary understandings have influenced common thinking. "Survival of the fittest" views have had their effects on morality, economics and social policy. The pastor dealing with the very human circumstances of suffering and evil does so in a world which, many would say, is controlled by impersonal physical laws in an indifferent and inherently meaningless process.

Haught continues in his preface: "Evolutionary science has changed our understanding of the world dramatically, and so any sense we may have of a God who creates and cares for this world must take into account what Darwin and his followers have told us about it. Although Darwin himself beheld a certain 'grandeur' in his new story of life, many of his scientific descendants, instead of taking his widening of the world's horizons as a springboard to a more exhilarating vision of God, have seen in evolution the final defeat of theism. Meanwhile, theology has generally failed to think about God in a manner proportionate to the opulence of evolution."

"A theology obsessed with order is ill-prepared for evolution," Haught writes later in his work. "But it is even less ready to embrace some of the more profound and disturbing aspects of religious experience itself, thus rendering it all the less capable of meaningful contact with the messiness of evolution. What makes evolution seem incompatible with the idea of God is not so much the startling Darwinian news about nature's struggle and strife, but theology's own failure to reflect deeply the divine pathos. What Darwin does — and this is part of his 'gift to theology' — is challenge religious thought to recapture the tragic aspects of divine creativity. Evolutionary science compels theology to reclaim features of religious faith that are all too easily smothered by the deadening disguise of order and design."

Throughout his book, Haught prods and probes as he offers insight into ways in which a theology that includes evolutionary understandings may become richer and more profound. "... (Darwin's) science, when not suffocated by the stale climate of a materialist metaphysics, can give considerable depth and richness to our sense of the great mystery into which our religions attempt to initiate us" (p. 5).

"In any case, the notion of God as an intelligent designer is inadequate. The God of evolution is an inexhaustible and unsettling source of new modes of being, forever eluding encapsulation in orderly schemata. Looking beneath the anxious quest for intelligent design, a theology of evolution seeks to highlight the disquieting — but ultimately fulfilling —

presence of a promise and power of renewal that lives, in Gerard Manley Hopkins' familiar words, 'deep down things'" (p. 9).

"God's empathy enfolds not just the human sphere but the whole of creation, and this can mean only that the vast evolutionary odyssey, with all of its travail, enjoyment, and creativity, is also God's own travail, enjoyment, and creativity. Nothing that occurs in evolution can appropriately be understood by faith and theology as taking place outside of God's own experience" (p. 51).

"Nature, after Darwin, is not a design but a promise. God's 'plan' if we continue to use the term, is not a blueprint but an envisagement of what the cosmos might become ... Such an interpretation does not destroy the cosmic hierarchy but by its openness to new being brings special significance to every epoch of nature's unfolding, including humanity's unique history in a still unfinished universe."

Bits

On waves in rippled space
Spirit broods, blowing
the stellar ash transformed
that bursts into living
dazzled knots in the flow,
genetic wording
to spiraled paragraphs,
logos informing.
From those light years away,
whirlwinding and code,
suffering awareness
creation unfold,
a semiotic world,
yet being told.

Called to Be
a Faithful Church

We who are many are one body for we all share in the same bread.
"It takes the whole world to know the whole gospel."

Having been asked to Chair the 1998 Lambeth Conference's group of two hundred bishops dealing with issues of pluralism and unity in the church and world, I provided this summary view of the subject. "Cultures and Communion" (see p. 121) expands on the themes.

A vital part of the calling of Jesus' disciples is to tell of the gospel to all people. From earliest days this was to be done not only in the language of the various peoples but in terms of their thought forms, customs and mores. Jesus himself likely spoke both Aramaic and Greek and was adept at talking about God's reign in images and stories which spoke of sowing and reaping, sheep and goats, fish and nets, masters and slaves, families, vineyards, courts, weddings, and dinner parties.

One of the first challenges facing many early Christians was to teach and share the gospel stories of and about Jesus in the varied circumstances of the larger Mediterranean world. These Christians experienced many challenges and sometimes controversy and disagreement in doing this. How far could they go, not only in translation into different tongues, but with this translation to imbed the faith in the customs and practices of the cultures so that the gospel might be fully heard and believed? What could faithfully be adopted from the religion of the native peoples? The challenges became no easier as Christianity spread to still other countries — sometimes then becoming intensely nationalistic, as well as locally experienced.

The other side of the challenge, of course, was how faithfully to present a gospel which would inevitably be controversial in and critical of any culture, seeking both to work through but also to transform lives and cultures. Slavery, prostitution, male privilege to the detriment of women and children, racism, caste systems, materialism, over-zealous patriotism, militarism, unbridled capitalism and economic injustice are examples of aspects of culture which Christianity has stood against.

When through merchants, soldiers and missionaries the Christian faith of the Church of England spread to many parts of the world, members of the growing Anglican Communion experienced a number of these challenges. As its practice became more and more diverse, and, as it faced the challenges of modernity at varied paces in different regions, additional questions and issues arose. What happens when some member churches ordain women and others do not? How should the Eucharist be celebrated in a culture where the drinking of wine may be frowned upon or wine may not even be available?

Always there has been the danger that a particular cultural expression of Christianity will be assumed to be privileged and to enshrine beliefs and practices in ways they must be for others. To the contrary, it has been said that Christianity, although it is never experienced apart from a culture, does not so much have a culture as it seeks cultures in which to be a living faith — a universal faith always seeking a unique expression.

Yet how much difference can be accepted and still maintain a Communion with a recognizable identity — especially in an age where many cultures and religions feel threatened by thorough-going relativism? What things are vital for the essentials as well as for the good of Christian life and practice?

Now all these issues are experienced in a global community — rapidly being further linked by movies and television, air transportation, multinational corporations and products, fax and e-mail. There are new commonalities, yet in many areas ethnicity, cultures and tribalism grow stronger. The gap widens between the well-off and the poor. In some places Christians are very much in a minority and may experience persecution. At the same time population movement means that many cultures can exist side-by-side within particular regions, as is true, for instance, in the Los Angeles area where more than four hundred identifiable ethnic groups are now found. In such a setting, hybrid and newer cultures are also formed. There are, moreover, other differences between young and old, rich and poor and those of moderate means within these cultures.

Under this general theme of diversity and identity in Christian life and witness, Section III of the Lambeth Conference is asked to reflect, not only on the broader issues, but on some of the specific aspects of them, such as what it means to be the body of Christ where through baptism all are called to ministry. What are the roles of deacons and of bishops, particularly of "bishops in synod"; that is, bishops together with representatives of all the people helping to lead the churches in mission and ministry? Marriage, family and sexuality, money, scriptural interpretation, spiritualities, liturgy, relations with other religions, and ways of doing theology will be other matters for study and reflection.

Together, the bishops in Conference will recognize that they represent some thirty-eight independent Churches in our Anglican Communion, a Communion which greatly values as part of Christian life and practice a sense of "dispersed authority." This is an authority shared by the people of God. It is an authority in which many voices can be heard — saints, the lowly as well as the strong — in which scripture, tradition and reasoning experience all have their roles. We are members of a Communion which recognizes the remarkable diversity of the early churches and the dynamism of the Christian faith which cannot be limited to one expression. For this reason every expression must be regarded as provisional. Diversity is valued for bringing a greater awareness of the fullness of the faith and the activity of God's Spirit.

We are held together as a communion in *koinonia* of the Spirit, not by a magisterium, but, by the common stories of our faith, by basic creeds, by worship and prayer, by the sacraments of baptism and eucharist, by memories of our saints and heroes, by together seeking to show forth the fruits of the Spirit in love and service, by recognizing our interdependence and the resources for sharing God has given us: thus, we establish and maintain bonds of mutual affection.

One of the principles to be discussed at Lambeth is that of subsidiarity, which views church councils as having assisting or supplementary roles and holds that matters of faith should usually be dealt with at the lowest or most local level possible. Yet the more local level is never understood as autonomous, and there will also be issues and concerns which call for more common study, planning, conversation, learning and agreement. From this perspective we shall be looking as well at what are called the "instruments" of Anglican unity: the convening role of the Archbishop of Canterbury, the Anglican Consultative Council, the Council of Primates, and the role of the Lambeth Conference itself.

We who are many are one body for we all share in the same bread.

Lambeth Learnings

This perspective on the Lambeth Conference of bishops, held in 1998 in Canterbury, England, was written shortly after the meeting.

Eight hundred bishops in one place are a lot of bishops. Eight hundred bishops from almost every part of the world (plus guests representing other churches and faiths) make for a sometimes confusing but often enriching three-week experience.

We knew ourselves to be representatives of a Communion of Anglican Churches now speaking many languages and called to worship and live out our Christian faith in a great variety of cultures. We rejoiced in that diversity while also being aware that a faithful Christianity will always challenge dehumanizing aspects of every culture. We also knew that we must not let "culture" become an excuse for lessening the sometimes counter-cultural challenge of Christian living.

We were aware of ourselves living in a time when cultural differences can drive people apart — emphasizing ethnicity, religion and even tribe and clan sometimes to the point of strife and warfare. Yet in this same world there are life-changing technological developments involving travel and communications. Movies, television, popular music and advertising, and the growing power of multinational corporations are leading to the homogenization of human experience at various levels. This has been called the McWorlding, McDonaldization, Disneyfication, and CocaCola-izing of the world — sometimes resulting in resentment, fear and efforts to protect distinctive cultural values. This changing experience is compounded by the increasing urbanization of societies and by population movements, the results of which are hybrid cultures and the differences around the world between "youth cultures" and those of their elders.

On a day-to-day basis, we were aware as well (for it was embodied in our midst) of the agonizing differences between the have-nots and the haves in our cultures. We live together in a world where 1.3 billion people try to exist on less than $1 a day, 8 million children die every year of diseases linked to impure water and air pollution, and 50 million more are mentally and physically damaged because of poor nutrition.

In this complex and challenging context, we spoke of our common faith as disciples of Jesus. We asked what held us together as a Communion or *koinonia* (community) of believers. We particularly valued the centrality of the Bible and the shared stories of our faith, the Apostles' and Nicene creeds, the sacraments of baptism and eucharist, the historic episcopate adapted in our different settings, and our common patterns of worship. We found ourselves to be joined in prayer by the communion of saints, the witness of the heroes and heroines of our history, by interdependence through exchanges of friendship between our dioceses and by service to others in the name of Christ.

We discussed the significance of the Anglican Consultative Council (now the Anglican Communion Council — a meeting every three years of lay and clergy representatives from the thirty-seven Churches or Provinces of the Communion), the Lambeth Conference itself, the role of the Archbishop of Canterbury, and the meeting of the thirty-seven primate bishops in helping us to know ourselves to be a Communion.

There were a number of shared experiences during those three weeks together, beginning with the vibrant opening worship service — complete with drums and dancing — in the ancient cathedral. We could then, day by day, view the great cathedral, set in the heart of the city of Canterbury, from the hillside on which the University of Kent, our home for those weeks, is located.

For the first time there were women bishops participating in the Conference. After all the fuss and feathers of ten years ago, they and their contributions were fully welcomed by the great majority of bishops. Meanwhile, their spouses and all the others were holding an interesting parallel conference. One of its features was their performance of a musical drama based on stories of Oscar Wilde, an irony not lost upon a number of us.

On forty buses, we went one afternoon to have tea with the Queen at

Buckingham Palace which certainly proved to us again that we were Anglicans. There was a day of vigil and fast in which we were guided in meditation by Jean Vanier, the leader of L'Arche — the movement which provides homes and community for the severely mentally and physically handicapped. Vanier spoke of seeing the beauty in the "weakest and least presentable members of the Body of Christ" and what we could come to share with one another.

On the feast day of the Transfiguration, remembering that August 6 is also the anniversary of the dropping of the first atomic bomb, we prayed about human disfiguration and the transfiguration of suffering. Our worship that day was led by the Church in Japan, which extended again its apology, not least to other Asian countries, for its complicity in the atrocities of the Second World War. We remembered all those who had died, including captive Koreans and others, at Hiroshima and Nagasaki. We prayed that no such bomb would ever annihilate again.

Then there were more individual stories, which we shared over meals and particularly in the intimacy of our daily Bible study groups. In my group there were three young African bishops, one from northern Nigeria (where Islam is strong), one from southern Malawi, and one from Ghana. Our convener was a white bishop from Pretoria in South Africa. There were two bishops from England, a Welsh bishop, another from impoverished Bangladesh, the Primate of the "Southern Cone" Province from northern Argentina, and a priest from Malaysia.

We heard stories of how the faithful attention to Scripture in South Africa brought about the courage and steadfastness to overcome the false use of the Bible and all the powers enforcing apartheid. We heard of converts to Christianity being given one week to abandon their faith or else lose all human rights and perhaps their lives. We were told of churches being burned by fundamentalist Muslims and of how one of our brothers and his family reached out to the Christians of another denomination even while their own church and home were burning. One of our group told of the death of his daughter in a car bombing. We learned how a poor diocese in South America took up collections to aid disciples in Rwanda. We groaned as we heard stories of churches ingrown on themselves, locked up in maintenance rather than mission. We laughed together as we admitted mistakes we had made, hard lessons learned in ministry, and we confessed our own shortsightedness and sin.

As the larger Conference proceeded, we discussed better ways of doing evangelism and mission, the mutual and shared ministry of every baptized disciple, and different forms and uses of ordained ministry. We deliberated about human rights, euthanasia, our common responsibility for environmental justice, and our relations with other churches and faiths.

The 1998 Lambeth Conference will probably best be known for its energy given to three issues: human sexuality, world debt, and relations with other faiths, particularly with Islam.

SEXUALITY

Notable were the widely different pastoral experiences between those bishops who were regularly involved in life and church work with gay and lesbian Christians and those who were not. Some bishops from Africa held that their cultures had no homosexuals. On the other hand, there was the witness of Desmond Tutu and others from South Africa of ministering with and to gay and lesbian persons in their churches.

Many were encouraged by the ways in which bishops in the subsection working on the volatile issue fought and argued, and then listened to one another, and ended with tears and embraces. There was no full common mind, but there was a good measure of agreement on upholding faithfulness in marriage between a man and a woman in life-long union, and in understanding this to be the place for the full expression of sexuality. They were unanimous in holding that some expressions of sexuality were contrary to the Christian way and sinful. They named "promiscuity, prostitution, incest, pornography, pedophilia, predatory sexual behavior, sadomasochism, adultery, violence against women and families, rape and female circumcision."

They agreed on the reality of the homosexual orientation and the place of all baptized and faithful persons, regardless of sexual orientation, as full members of the Body of Christ. They called upon all church members to work to end any discrimination on the basis of sexual orientation and to oppose homophobia. To the resolution on the subject was later added a commitment by all bishops to listen to the experience of homosexual persons.

When the resolution came to the full Conference plenary for debate and vote, many of the bishops who then spoke and voted had not been part of the earlier two-week process. While accepting much of the original resolution, they were concerned to let others know how any measure of countenance of homosexual practice by some churches was causing consternation in their churches and problems with other religions. They wanted to be sure that "This Conference... cannot advise the legitimizing or blessing of same sex unions or ordaining those involved in same gender unions." This was the view of a considerable majority of the bishops. The character and tone of some of the debate was unfortunate and made one wonder about the commitment to listen to others and to respect their place as full members of the Body of Christ.

A constant subtext in the debate had to do with the authority and interpretation of Scripture. For some this was, they held, the larger issue. A number of bishops, especially from Africa, felt that too much interpretation of the Bible was a reason for poor evangelism, while their more "plain sense" way of using Scripture in their cultural settings was helping their churches to grow. Some of this discussion was a little surprising to those who knew earlier Lambeth Conference statements on the necessity and value of wise and Spirit-led interpretation of Scripture in the contemporary world. One had to wonder if the concern for "rejecting homosexual practice as incompatible with Scripture" (words also added to the original resolution) was not a kind of tail wagging the dog.

Two days after the debate, the esteemed Primate of Central Africa delivered a strong homily which included these words directed to some of his colleagues in Africa and beyond. "The tenor of [some of our discussions] can only be described as 'frenzied.' The tone in which they were expressed was devoid of the love of God. We have had tyrants using the Bible as armor and words spoken from this very spot which were aimed to wound and score debating points.... I want to say here and now, I have resisted tyranny all my life and nor will I ever tolerate it from those who claim the love of the Bible over everyone else. Let not the intolerance of a variety of contexts inexorably lead us to intolerance, which, if unchecked, will find us with a band of vigilantes and fundamentalists."

Another subtext in the debate, which was evident at other points in the Conference, was a more general concern about a materialist, commercializing, individualistic "western" culture (of which divorce, selfish sexual gratification and homosexuality were sometimes seen as parts) and a need to struggle against its intrusiveness. There was, too, a measure of anti-colonialism still evident in the Communion. From this perspective one found a sense of new leadership in the Communion from the now majority bishops of newer and mostly "southern" (in the sense of southern hemisphere and near the equator) dioceses.

While I was disappointed in the final form of the resolution and the character of parts of the debate (as well as the heavy politicking around it — ironically aided by "western" money and direction — although some doubtless felt it justified because of the importance of their goal), there were positive gains as well. For a number of bishops this was their first opportunity to discuss the issue and to hear of the reality of faithful and committed disciples of Jesus who are gay and lesbian. It was their first chance to learn of the kinds of discrimination and sometimes persecution these Christians had and were experiencing. In turn, these bishops were also right to help others see more clearly the brokenness around much of the sexual fascination and expression in western cultures, although this is sadly and often tragically also true in different ways in their own settings. We knew again that every Christian is called and challenged to a faithful dedication of sexuality as in all other areas of life.

What yet has to be worked out is all of what it means to regard "all baptized, believing and faithful persons, regardless of sexual orientation, as full members of the Body of Christ" and what will happen as the result of all bishops committing themselves "to listen to the experience of homosexual persons," and what this then will mean for their pastoral understanding and experience. In the meantime, as with the stories of the full incorporation of gentiles, women, Blacks and others into the life of the Body, one cannot believe that for those churches which have already experienced the full inclusion of gay and lesbian followers of Jesus will there be any going back.

WORLD DEBT

The natural inclination of many of us is to say that all debts must be paid. But what if the debt was incurred by a previously corrupt regime supported by western powers during the cold war? What if some of the debt paid for a tank which attacked your parents? What if the interest paid on the debt is now quite a bit more than the equivalent of the principal? What if the interest on the debt is more than is being spent on a nation's health care and education for their children? What if the structure of the debt has helped to create long-standing trade imbalances favoring richer countries? If individuals and corporations can declare that they no longer can pay their debts, what about an impoverished country?

Take Mozambique, one of the poorest of the forty-one countries which the World Bank and the International Monetary Fund have identified as Heavily Indebted Poor Countries (HIPCs). Mozambique owes fifty percent of its annual national budget to interest on its loans. The debt for each person is $223 while the average annual income is $80. Mozambique's government spends about twice as much on debt payments as on education and four times as much as on health care.

The issues are complicated and debt relief alone will not solve the problems. Desmond Tutu is among those who have called on debtor nations to meet four conditions before receiving debt relief: democratization (and, one many add, an attack on corruption), respect for human rights, military reduction, and a commitment to use the money gained from debt relief for the needs of ordinary people.

The total owed by the HIPCs is $214 billion — not really a huge sum when compared to what was needed to bail out the savings and loans' crisis in this country or what will be needed to rescue Japanese banks. It is small when compared to the USA's $5.4 trillion debt, although only a relatively small portion of HIPC debt is owed to the United States and its banks which is among the reasons why international cooperation and effort are called for.

The bishops of the Lambeth Conference have declared their belief that it is moral and of benefit for the whole world community that all of the international debt of the poorest countries be cancelled as part of the

Jubilee 2000 campaign. The bishops have collectively set out their willingness to work with other religious groups, organizations and countries toward this goal.

RELATIONS WITH ISLAM

The Lambeth Conference heard how Christian relations with Islamic peoples vary considerably. Some bishops spoke of cooperative work and dialogue. But bishops from Pakistan, the Sudan, Nigeria and several other countries told hair-raising stories of persecution and martyrdom. The Conference spent considerable time on the issues, and recognized past Christian sins and the historic contribution of Islamic culture to ideals of justice and religious freedom. It resolved to support the civil and religious liberties of Muslims where they are a minority, and to combat prejudice and ignorance about Islam among Christians and others.

Affirming the right of Christians to present their faith and witness (so recognizing the responsibility of Christians to be able to present their faith authentically), the Conference set forth its belief that God is the God of all people. God's Spirit is in all the world. In this light, the bishops called for continuing dialogue with all religions, a shared commitment to non-violence, care for the environment, and common good works for the benefit of others. It asked for those of other faiths to stress the charity and benevolence at the heart of their religions and that they affirm the right of all people to freedom of worship and the practice of their faith.

As we boarded the buses and trains taking us from Canterbury and the 13th Lambeth Conference, there was an awareness that many of us who had worshiped and prayed together, shared something of each others' faith and experience and become friends, would likely not see one another again in this life. In any event, ten years is a long time to wait for another conference, even if one would be eligible to return in 2008.

We were aware of the varied circumstances and challenges to which we were returning and some of the pain and differences we had found among ourselves. There was again the question: What makes us a communion? What holds our churches together?

It can only be the call of the Spirit, inviting and challenging us to faithful worship, to humility, the learning of the love of Jesus with one another, and to service. I continue to hear the songs of our worship in many languages:

Santo, santo, santo / Mi corazón te adora
Mi corazón te sabe decir / Santo eres Señor

Cultures and Communion:

Diversity and Commonality in the Church and in the World

The Bishop Gray Memorial Lecture presented at the University of Cape Town, South Africa, on September 4, 2001, develops themes of pluralism and a shared humanity from the meeting of bishops from around the world at the 1998 Lambeth Conference.

It is a privilege to be invited to present this Bishop Gray Memorial Lecture. In recent months I have been interested to read of the beginnings of the mission of the Anglican Church in South Africa and of Bishop Gray's arrival in Cape Town in 1848, followed by the years of his pioneering ministry. I could not help but note some parallels with early mission and ministry in my country, as well as many differences.

Although there was a considerable population of peoples native to North America when the first European settlers came, and some notable efforts were made to bring the gospel of Jesus Christ to them, there is mostly a sad history of devastating diseases, the taking of lands and a consequent dwindling of Native American peoples. While I am grateful to report that a number of Native Americans are Christians today, there are yet considerable poverty and societal problems. This, together with the results of the myth that white settlers were moving into "empty country," and the smaller numbers of Native Americans, has meant that the history of the development of North America has, for the most part, largely excluded the land's original inhabitants.

The relationship of those early colonists from Europe and the succeeding generations with England was complicated. There was the often arduous and dangerous sea voyage that separated America from England, giving rise to difficulties with communications and understanding that eventually led to the War of Independence and a new country of thirteen states coming together as the United States of America. The fledgling Church of England, strong particularly in the middle-Atlantic States from Connecticut through the Carolinas, found itself in difficult straits after the war. A number of the laity and more than half of the clergy had been loyal to England during the revolution. Quite a few of them left for Canada when England lost the war. The weakened Church was struggling for an identity. Who were they now that the political connection with the home country and its support was broken? Moreover, the Church in the United States had no bishops. In the past clergy had come from England or had gone there to be ordained before returning to minister in the new country. Were bishops even needed? And, it was asked, what kind of bishops would there be, since many Virginians and New Yorkers, among others, remembered or had been told about English bishops who were prelates linked with the upper class and indifferent to the needs of their flock. In the end, the episcopate came to the United States through the Non-Juring bishops of the Episcopal Church in Scotland. Two results of this derivation were the Church's name as the Protestant Episcopal Church in the United States of America and the acceptance of the Scottish form for the celebration of the Holy Eucharist.

The unique history of this early development of an offshoot of the Church of England in the United States is, however, in its way typical for each of the thirty-eight member churches of the Anglican Communion throughout the world. Each of them has a different and special story because they began in different lands at somewhat different times and among different people and circumstances. These diversities of cultures and languages profoundly affected the ways in which the Christian faith of the Church of England come to be presented, interpreted and practiced in many areas of the world.

As the eight hundred or so bishops of the Anglican Communion prepared to gather in Canterbury, England, for the Lambeth Conference of 1998, the recognition of this pluralism influenced planning for one of the major discussions of the Conference, and I was asked to chair the Section entitled "Called to Be a Faithful Church in a Plural World." Diversity, we realized, is not only part of our history but is also of great significance in our contemporary churches and in the many countries and cultures of the Communion. Furthermore, the many different influences are playing themselves out in a world of rapid change and development. A number of these developments are also bringing with them countervailing pressures toward homogeneity. Transnational forces, carried by the growing influence of music, movies, radio, television and the Internet, are fueled by the advertising money of large corporations leading to what has been called the Disneyfying, the Cocacolization and McDonaldization of the world. Billions of people know Mickey Mouse (from my Los Angeles) and now Michael Jordan and Michael Jackson and maybe even someone like the notorious Al Capone. When I was traveling in remote areas of the former Yugoslavia some years ago, and would tell people that I was born and raised in Chicago, they responded by setting their arms as though they were holding a sub-machine gun and making an ek-ek-ek-ek sound. They knew of the Chicago gangster from the movies they had seen.

On the cover of a book entitled *Jihad and McWorld: How Globalism and Tribalism Are Reshaping the World* (by Benjamin R. Barber), there is one of those pictures that says more than a thousand words. A Muslim woman, covered otherwise from head to toe in her black garments, peers out at the world with bright young eyes. In her hand she holds a can of Pepsi-Cola. Almost everywhere the commercial forces penetrate — influencing the shoes and shirts that are worn, the music that is heard, changes in language and values. The forces are threatening to those concerned to preserve the values of their own cultures. In some regions, the response has been a religious-cultural fundamentalism. But wherever these forces penetrate, sometimes carrying with them a breath of freedom of choice and forms of democracy, they seem irresistible — especially to the young. Offering at least the possibility of the benefits of technological and informational development, the forces also bear with them materialistic values and the values of a consumerist individualism that more communal societies find suspect. To other societies, the western exaltation of individual rights may seem to emphasize the right of individuals to assert their needs and wants over the values of the common good. It is indeed, a complex movement and interaction of products and ideas.

The thirty-eight churches of the Anglican Communion find themselves trying to teach and practice their Christian faith among all these mixed and mixing influences. Moreover, due to greater migration and opportunities for travel, each of these societies is becoming increasingly hybridized. Los Angeles, where I live and minister, is far from alone in this, but it does lead the way. In the most diverse region the world has ever known there are some two hundred and forty distinctive ethnic groups of more than ten thousand persons. Salvadorean and Armenian, people from Mexico, Korea, and the Philippines, along with other groups by the hundreds of thousands and millions live in the region. Children in the public school system come from homes where, collectively, nearly two hundred languages are spoken. In our Episcopal churches, one finds Asian and Hispanic peoples, people from the Middle East and Belize, Ghana, Nigeria, Uganda and South Africa, along with American Blacks and the no-longer majority population of people of European ancestry. We are, I should think, the most diverse diocese in the Anglican Communion. In each of these cultural groups, moreover, one can see how the values and concerns of the younger people differ from those of parents and grandparents. Each of these groups has a youth culture no longer speaking the language of their elders. And, more and more, Chinese marries Filipino, Japanese marries Caucasian, American Black marries a person from Africa, a Nigerian marries someone from Puerto Rico, and on it goes.

But again, what is happening in Los Angeles is just the leading edge of what is taking place in other places and is an important indication of the world's future. Certainly it is a reality in South Africa, a land of eleven official languages. Here there has been a long history of immigration and migration, the mixing of races and peoples. Many newcomers still continue to come, especially from other parts of Africa. They bring the enterprise and gifts of their own cultures, but also challenges and conflict in circumstances where there is severe poverty and lack of employment. Here, as in Los Angeles, there are gay and lesbian persons. There are cultural, theological and economic differences that make it difficult, certainly even in our churches, to be fully "the rainbow people of God."

How does one best share the Christian faith in such circumstances? In what measures and ways should the teaching and practices of the faith be adapted for and indigenized in the different cultures? What also are the dangers? In what ways may the values and virtues of Christian faith be overwhelmed by cultural ideas and practices such as materialism, nationalism, slavery, racism, classism, and sexism against which Christianity should set itself?

In trying to address these questions in the modern world, the bishops gathered at Lambeth also realized that, while we are, of course, dealing with circumstances that are modern and contemporary, the questions, in one form or another, are as old as Christianity. In the first place, it is important to realize that faith has always come enmeshed in a cultural context. The Christian faith has never existed apart from a living setting of language and a host of values and understandings having to do with family, kin, sex, gender relations, authority, money, food and God.

Christian faith first took root in the variegated population of the occupied land of the Jewish people where there were differences of living circumstances and religious practice between Jerusalem and the Galilee, among the Essenes and the newly urbanized cities of Sepphoris and Tiberias. Judaism itself had already experienced influences from other religions and philosophies in the region.

The growing use of currency was affecting the economy and creating a new kind of poverty for those with few or no coins to buy necessities. Changing economic circumstances may have been among the reasons why Jesus' words about looking for security in God alone found hearing.

Remarkable in the recollection of Jesus' teaching are the ways he was remembered to have used images and stories of everyday circumstances to tell of how God's kingdom — the ways of God — could already be experienced. He spoke of seeds and sowing and reaping, sheep and goats, fish and nets, masters and slaves, families, vineyards, courts, weddings, and dinner parties. The variety of these images and their everyday character has served subsequent Christians as an encouragement and reminder that for faith to flourish in other lands and times it must also be rooted in the circumstances of mundane life. It cannot just be some special area of life called religion or the spiritual that might be practiced in some pristine condition apart from the warp and woof of daily living.

The Galilean Jesus evidently encountered people of different cultures and may well have spoken both Aramaic and Greek. After his death, the story of Pentecost relates how the resurrection faith, empowered by the Spirit of Jesus, broke through barriers of languages. With different languages, of course, came differences of customs and understanding as well. It is often noted, for instance, that the Greek language of the New Testament has at least four words that are all translated by the one English word *love*.

Some of the changes that resulted were, no doubt spontaneous adaptations. I have illustrated this for my beginning New Testament students by comparing the story of the healing of the paralytic in the Gospels of Mark and Luke. In order to bypass the crowd and bring the paralyzed man to Jesus, his four friends, we are told, unroofed a portion of the house by digging through what would have been a hard dirt covering and pulling apart the branches and matting on which it was laid. Luke, however, telling the story to a people who had tile roofs, has the friends lower the bed down "through the tiles." This illustration may seem trivial, but, multiplied many times over in narrative and basic views, needs and understandings, it yields Gospels as different as Matthew's from John's and letters as diverse as that of James and the Epistle to the Hebrews. The diversity in the scriptures committed Christianity to an openness and dynamism in expression of faith and practice, even though, perhaps understandably, there have always been efforts to try to freeze a version of Christianity in time and to say this is how it has always been and will always be. The evangelical character of Christianity — the urge to make new disciples in different and changing circumstances — has regularly, however, even if unintentionally, warmed the frozen versions causing new adaptations.

But not without controversy. How far could people go in imbedding the faith in the customs and practices of others so that the Gospel might be fully heard and believed? In the early years, the requirement of circumcision and much of the Jewish dietary law were let go so that Gentiles could be fully included. Concepts of Greek philosophy were used for the language of the creeds. Later features from other cultures were adopted and adapted for the observance of Christmas and Lent. When we view fifteen or 16th century Italian paintings of biblical scenes, or those of the Dutch of 17th century, we may smile at their depictions of the clothes and landscapes, their versions of first century garb and backgrounds heavily influenced by their own. But it was ever thus. Pictures of Jesus himself have gone from Semitic to Greek, to Slavic and Scandinavian. He has become Black and Asiatic. Depictions of a female corpus on the cross and discussions of Jesus being a homosexual, however scandalous to some, are only the latest efforts to say that Jesus is of us and for us.

So again, it is asked, how far can people go in indigenizing and embedding without losing some essentials of what Christianity is all about? Are there not aspects of Christianity that transcend culture and, for that matter, that may be critical of values and practices of every culture? Cannot "this is our culture," "this is the way we do things," become an excuse for a less challenging and demanding form of faith?

In an influential book, *Christ and Culture* written in 1951, H. Richard Niebuhr reflected on the various ways faith could relate to culture, becoming fully part of it, but yet challenging and seeking to transform it as well. These themes were more recently studied and discussed from a variety of perspectives at a conference on world mission and evangelism that took place in Salvador, Brazil, in 1996, and in its record and reports *Called to One Hope — The Gospel in Diverse Cultures* (edited by Christopher Duraisingh). The message of the conference holds that it is the church's mission to be involved in

> *Every aspect of life in a rapidly changing world of many cultures now interacting and overlapping... The gospel, to be most fruitful, needs to be both true to itself and incarnated or rooted in the culture of people... We need constantly to seek the insight of the Holy Spirit in helping us better to discern where the gospel challenges, endorses or transforms a particular culture.*

In the history of Christianity, forms of cultural imperialism and nationalism stand out as ways in which a faithful Christianity has been subverted and then used by the culture. Militarism, wars, xenophobia and racism have been sanctioned instead of challenged. Slavery, prostitution, and male privilege to the detriment of women and children; caste systems, materialism, unbridled capitalism and economic injustice are all features of culture against which Christianity has had to stand or should have been opposed. Cultural values are never all good, even though many a culture has wanted to think of itself as the best.

In the story of the spread of Christianity, there has frequently been a tendency by the dominant culture to present its version of Christianity as the best if not virtually the only one. In the last hundred years or so, the history of this tendency has been made more evident as African and Asian cultures have reinterpreted aspects of Christian faith expressed in categories that come ultimately from Greek philosophy. Established conceptions of church order and authority have also been challenged. In still more controversial efforts to imbed the faith locally, the possibility has been raised that indigenous religious beliefs and stories might augment the Hebrew Scriptures as the background for Christian belief in African and non-western cultures.

Those of us whose faith came originally from the Church of England have our own stories to tell about an English version of the Christian faith being presented as the best. We may be entertained now by some of these stories as we recognize that it is hard for any group of people, especially before the revolutions in the means of transportation and information sharing, to see their own culture as a culture. One's culture is instead, something like water for the fish, the way things are and have to be. It can be compared to how we speak our language. You all have English accents. I don't.

In England, as some of us well know, the weather is often chilly. Churches can be cold. People wear clothes to church, sometimes a lot of them. An older colleague of mine in an English theological college wore a hot water bottle under his cloak to morning chapel. When it came time for English missionaries to preach the gospel in tropical climes where people wore fewer clothes (sometime, from an English perspective, too few clothes), one of the first overtures of the missionaries was, "put on some clothes, and we will teach you how to be Christians." "Christians get dressed up."

Or it could be utensils. Years ago my family invited a priest from South India to be our guest for a holiday dinner. He asked if we would mind if he ate the meal with his fingers, as that was his custom. The eyes of my three young sons nearly fell out of their heads as all they could remember their parents saying in this regard was, "Don't play with your food. Don't touch your food! Use your spoon; use your fork." The priest noted to us that approximately a third of the world eats with knife, fork and spoon, a third with chopsticks, and a third with hands and fingers. He then proceeded to eat his dinner using bread and his fingers in a decorous manner, much to my sons' delight and fascination.

But from the perspective of English missionaries, it was, at least at first, part of the opportunity and burden of bringing Christian civilization to others to teach them how to use *proper* utensils. Moreover, it may have been hard for some of the early converts not to think that the use of utensils was anything but part of being a proper, civilized Christian.

Sometime in 1986, Desmond Tutu and I were at a meeting in Lambeth Palace as part of the planning team for the 1988 Lambeth Conference. He had asked to see Prime Minister Thatcher while he was in London to talk about apartheid and divestiture, and she wanted to see him as well. He left our meeting in the early afternoon to go to 10 Downing Street and returned at suppertime. We were, of course, eager to hear what had transpired. "Well," he said, "at first she wasn't quite ready for us, so we were given some tea. Then we were ushered into her office and given tea again. You know, I think tea is an English weapon."

The stories extend, of course, to the style of church buildings, to "Christian names," to liturgies and music. But gradually over the years, it has come to be all right to share the gospel in different clothes, buildings, with new liturgies and in local rhythms and tunes as signs that Christianity, fully to be Christianity, must speak to people in their everyday circumstances and lives. In these and many other modes of custom and thought, it is now seen as not only good but necessary for Christianity to engage with every aspect of a society's culture. One of the more interesting discussions at the Lambeth Conference involved the principle of "subsidiarity" — a recognition that central organization and authority "should have a subsidiary function, performing only those tasks which cannot be performed effectively at a more immediate and local level." (This definition is from the *Oxford English Dictionary*.) Many decisions and interactions with local culture are best left to the local churches.

But again questions arise as diversity grows. Purportedly at the 1978 Lambeth Conference, an older English bishop arose and asked in a voice more sad than querulous, "What now holds the Anglican Communion together? We used to have English as a common language. Now many languages are used. We once had a common liturgy. Now there are all sorts of adaptations and new prayer books. We used to have a common ministry. Now some among us are even ordaining women. What holds the Communion together?" After a longish silence an African bishop, seeking to bring some humor to the situation, responded "Wippell's" — Wippell's, of course, being the English ecclesiastical clothier known through much of the Communion — not least to bishops.

Bishops laughed in 1978, but the questions have remained, and, from time to time, there have been renewed efforts to identify and give definition to what could be regarded as the essentials of Christian faith and practice apart from any cultural influences. What came to be called the Lambeth Quadrilateral is one of best known of these efforts:

A. The Holy Scriptures of the Old and New Testaments, as "containing all things necessary to salvation and as being the rule and ultimate standard of faith.

B. The Apostles Creed, as the Baptismal Symbol; and the Nicene Creed, as the sufficient statement of the Christian Faith.

C. The two Sacraments ordained by Christ Himself — Baptism and the Supper of the Lord — ministered with unfailing use of Christ's Words of Institution, and elements ordained by Him.

D. The Historic Episcopate, locally adapted in the methods of its administration to the varying needs of the nations and people called of God into the Unity of the Church.

The Quadrilateral may be helpful insofar as it goes, but it evidently does not go far enough. More questions and concerns arise. How far can the episcopate be adapted? How are the Creeds to be used and interpreted? The Quadrilateral does not say anything about lay presiders at the Eucharist. What should happen at the Eucharist in cultures where wine is frowned upon or hard to come by? Where bread is not a staple? And Scripture! Is not some good measure of agreed interpretation and use of scripture fundamental to the sharing of a common Christianity? What, the Communion has certainly been at great pains to debate, should be said to gay and lesbian Christians? When Anglican Christianity maintains that the

Holy Scriptures contain "all things necessary to salvation," in how minimalist a manner might this dictum be understood?

Attempts are sometimes made to distinguish the essence of faith and practice from what is called the *bene esse* — what is, in addition, good and helpful to the expression and practice of the faith. There is also the *plene esse* or a full and complete expression. Perhaps the *esse* could be defined as essential to the one, holy, catholic and apostolic church while there could be more adaptation regarding what is beneficial and of the fullness. But, of course, differences arise over what belongs in each category. How about the episcopate? Are bishops really absolutely necessary to the faith?

There are, of course, many more aspects and nuances to questions like these, and they are further compounded when we recognize again that there never has been or, for that matter, could there be a version of Christianity apart from a culture. This makes it virtually impossible to say what some essential Christianity apart from culture would look like.

The 1998 Lambeth Conference and earlier reports and meetings have spoken again of scripture, the creeds, sacraments and episcopate of the Quadrilateral in the light of a trinitarian faith as fundamental elements of unity. These are augmented by a commitment to prayer and worship and the spiritual life, a common theological methodology grounded in Scripture, tradition and reason, by bonds of affection among Anglicans throughout the world, by aspects of church history that are in the background of all our churches, by stories of heroes and saints of the faith that can be shared, and by a common sense of service and servant ministry. Four "instruments" that help link the Communion – the Archbishop of Canterbury, the Lambeth Conference, the Primates' meetings and the Anglican Communion Council —were also given a further role and definition at the 1998 Conference.

My purpose here, however, is not to try to set forth the articles that hold the Anglican Communion together so much as to recognize the strong feeling that it does and should continue a Communion. Efforts at defining and even arguing about theological and ecclesiastical essentials for churches to be in full communion will go forward. Perhaps it makes sense, however to recognize that there are always things which distinguish and to some degree divide peoples, and that being in full communion is always a goal and is experienced as a journey and process to that goal — toward the mystical unity of which Jesus spoke in John's Gospel "so that they may be one, as we are one" (17.11).

This is not to say that the discussions about unity, links and essentials are not useful. They are, but there is, I believe, something deeper and more profound happening. There is the awareness that we need one another, that we share a common humanity with many of the same fears and hopes, and that together we have a need to love and be loved. We are discovering that we may come better to know our own humanity by responding to the full humanity of others, while we are responding to a love we believe God has shown and shows to us in a world still often perilous with sin and suffering. I do not want to exaggerate the role of prayer and the help and support that were given, but, when you fought your heroic battles against the evils of apartheid, it was important for many of you to be part of the Anglican Communion. As I and others in the United States ask how we can deal with continuing racism at home and abroad, become a fairer and more generous people in the world, struggle to protect the environment and avoid being overcome by materialism, our small but potentially influential church needs your guidance, Christian wisdom and prayers. How ought we, for instance, best respond to the United Nations Conference on Racism now being held in Durban?

When one asks what it is that Christianity can most give and share with others in our world it is perhaps this awareness of a common humanity, all equally loved by God and in need of love for self and one another. At the same time it is also part of our common humanity to have differences. Diversities among people and cultures will continue, and we do not want to lose what we treasure and value among our differences, for from such differences we can learn from one another and complement one another. The proverb that "it takes the whole world to know the whole gospel" reminds us of all that we have to gain by affirming our differences in ways that are enriching for our humanity and our understanding of what it means for us to be created in the image of God. Moreover, it will always be in our particular settings and circumstances that we hear and seek to live in the ways of our faith.

While we together recognize some of the forces toward homogeneity that are threatening what is good in different cultures, we can also give thanks for a number of benefits. When I first became bishop in Los Angeles, it took at least several weeks to exchange letters with bishop friends in Africa. Soon came the facsimile machine, and if there was not a machine at diocesan headquarters in Kenya, Ghana, or South Africa, there usually was one not far away. Messages were exchanged in a day or two. Now with some of you I have been on the Internet using e-mail back and forth on a regular basis in preparation for this visit.

I do not know how many weeks it took Bishop Gray to reach Cape Town, but Barbara and I flew here from Los Angeles in little more than a day. Mind you. Bishop Gray was probably more rested when he arrived, but we could not have come if the round-trip journey took months.

For at least many of us, travel and information are much more readily shared. We can know each other and of each other in ways impossible until recently. The World Wide Web and Internet bring about opportunities for a much greater democratization of information. We can give thanks for more productive ways of growing food and for modern medicine, even while we must be determined to see that its benefits can be more widely and fairly shared — not least now in the fearful struggle with HIV/AIDS.

Other technological advances provide for the possibilities of greater economic development and world trade and exchange that could benefit all. At the same time there are certainly inherent dangers that could continue to bring about economic domination, global environmental deterioration, and a grossly unbalanced economic order. Transnational advertising would like us all to become consumers who wear similar shoes, while humming the same tunes, watching the same television, eating the same fast foods and drinking the same colas. It is economic and cultural domination, primarily through the imbalances of world trade, that protestors have been so vociferous in opposing at meetings of the leaders of the big eight countries, the World Trade Organization, World Bank and International Monetary Fund.

The facts of the matter are that we live in an increasingly complex world. Some basics of our humanity and human experience are little changed, but we are more aware than ever of our differences and heritages and want to cherish and make use of all that is of value in them. At the same time, through technology, information sharing and commercialism there are an increasing number of aspects of life that affect us all, some for good, some potential for good, some we could do much better without. The competition of globalism with regional and local cultures is bound to continue, and in all this, there is the opportunity to recognize how much we do share together in a common humanity. For those who are Christians together, there is also the opportunity to augment this awareness with a deeper sense of communion and responsibility one toward another. That sense of communality, of commonality and communion, of a greater *ubuntu*, can allow us to celebrate diversity without letting differences frighten us or cut us off from one another. It can make us be determined to use new ways of technology, manufacturing and information sharing to influence a world order that will allow for a better life of opportunity for all people. If I were to ask for one sign, above all, that these beneficial changes were beginning to happen, I would look for it in less money and resources being spent throughout the world on weapons and more on the development of the necessities and resources of life for people everywhere. In the year 2000, the so-called developing nations of the world spent more than twenty-five billion dollars buying weapons from the developed countries, the United States first, then Russia and Japan leading the way.

At a more local and practical level, many of the world's poor would be helped immensely if the laws of their countries would enable them to have clear title to property and assets in order to sell and buy and obtain loans. In this way, they could have liquid capital so that through their energy and ingenuity they might build stronger local economies and markets. (See Hernando de Soto's *The Other Path* and *The Mystery of Capital*.) A still more immediate step of great consequence would be further progress in canceling the onerous international debt that severely burdens the economies of a number of the world's poorest countries — a step urged by, among others, the Lambeth Conference, the Episcopal Church in the United States and championed by Archbishop Ndungane.

The world we live in places many of its hopes in technology and commercialization. Technology and world markets, it is hoped, will save us from our gross economic disparities, the looming shortage of water in many parts of the world, and from environmental degradation even while a considerable amount of this progress — not least over the last twenty years — points in reverse directions. Better education for more people is another hope that many can share in and support, although good education is yet to be widespread or effective enough to fulfill its promise, much less to change hearts. Nor has Christianity, at least in my country other than sporadically, lived very far up to its hope of fashioning a wiser, more generous and service-minded people. Perhaps what we most have to share in common in today's world of diversities and conformities is a profound and painful awareness that gross disparities of opportunity for human beings in our world continue. There are many historical, geographical and other reasons for these disparities, but there remains an injustice and suffering that our sense of common humanity and our faith call us, at the very least, to seek to alleviate. We are again reminded that there is always a moral dimension to the economic order — that help for those with the fewest opportunities always depends on some measure of restraint on the part of the more privileged. The economy is never just a naturalistic, mechanistic order, but rather part of an *oikinomia* of shared human decision. A healthy *oikinomia* and economy call for the careful and caring management of wealth and resources with the avoidance of waste, environmental damage, and gross distortions, dislocations and dominations. In a number of instances people-oriented governments need to find more courage and determination to control the impersonal, profit motives of transnational corporations and the sudden shifting of huge capital funds for short-term financial gains. When we talk of human rights, must we not also ask about the basic economic rights to food, housing and medical care that are in many ways prior to civil and political rights?

It may be that we only have the hope that these things can be done, but we need that hope if we are to continue to try to find the will, the intelligence, the compassion and generosity better to share what we have one with another — with and beyond our differences — through our churches and in our world. Hope may sometimes seem a weak foundation on which to build, but, as Paul reminds us (Romans 5: 3-5), a genuine and committed hope comes from a suffering that produces endurance. This endurance makes for character that then produces hope that will not disappoint because God's love has been poured into our hearts through the Holy Spirit. This is the ultimate hope that brings courage and the encouragement to continue to share with and support one another through both words of hope and encouragement and our ministries of service amid all our differences and in our commonality.

Warranted Faith

Holmes Rolston III is professor of philosophy at Colorado State University. I have learned much from his writings. Three of his books I have particularly valued are *Science and Religion: A Critical Survey* (Random House: 1987); *Environmental Ethics: Duties to and Values in The Natural World* (Temple University Press: 1988); and *Genes, Genesis and God: Values and their Origins in Natural and Human History*, the 1997-1998 Gifford Lectures (Cambridge University Press: 1999). The subject matter of these books deals with some of life's most profound questions. Rolston, whose understanding of science, philosophy and theology runs deep, writes clearly and well.

In *Environmental Ethics*, he asks about our responsibilities not only to other humans who live with us in our ecosystem and those who will come after, but to all of creation. What an irony it would be, he notes, if, with its intelligence and awareness "the sole moral species acts only in its collective self-interest to all the rest" (p.144). "Ought not this sole moral species do something less self-interested than count all the products of an evolutionary ecosystem as rivets in their spaceship, resources in their larder, laboratory materials, recreation for their ride?" (p. 157).

In *Science and Religion*, he examines the role of religion in life. "The task of religion is to examine that self in its relationships with the world, unmasking illusions and false cares, reforming it from self-centeredness, centering it on that which is of ultimate worth. This is worship, produced out of and returning to reflection. This worship, conceived as the self-disengagement from private concerns and engagement with the absolute, is precisely that universal intent that makes logic possible. Only such enthusiasm, or divine inspiriting, can get the self off-centered enough to reason right." (*Science and Religion*, p. 31).

"In John Keats' poetic phrase, not dislodged by science, the planetary space is a 'vale of soul-making.' If this is nature's chief beauty, then any elements of ordeal in nature have to be assessed against their contribution to soul making. Everywhere the ladder of ascent is climbed by problem solving. Nature produces a thesis, then an antithesis to it, and the result is a higher synthesis. Upward on the scale, joy and success come in counterpoint to agony and failure. The outcome is the dramatic quest for meaningful life" (*Science and Religion*, p. 244).

Rolston develops his thoughts regarding faith and evolutionary biology and psychology in *Genes, Genesis and God*: "...there are forms of creativity available in the sciences that are impossible genetically.... The result in the sciences is a vastly intensified and even radically novel capacity for creativity, for making discoveries of value. A vital component of this is the way in which ideas can be communicated socially, flow back and forth in feedback loops, with their value being evaluated by self-consciously critical communities, any acquired and worthwhile ideas transmitted to others, kindred or not, and to future generations, kindred or not. In terms of our larger paradigm, there is 'sharing' ('distribution,' 'dissemination,' 'multiplication,' 'reproduction') of such ideas and benefits that result, certainly something more than 'selfish genes' programming an organism to maximize its offspring" (*Genes, Genesis and God*, p. 180).

"God is an explanatory dimension for which contemporary biology leaves ample space, as we have seen biologists stutter over the origins of the information that generates complexity and diversity, over any selection for progress, over what to make of randomness, over the introduction of possibilities. If one adds the desire of a Creator not so much to conceal such complementing selective activities as to optimize the integrity, autonomy and self-creativity of the creatures — letting them do their thing, generating and testing, discarding what does not work and keeping what does — with divine coaching on occasion, then a conclusion that there is a divine presence underneath natural history becomes as plausible as there is not. The question becomes not so much a matter of conclusive proof as of warranted faith"(*Genes, Genesis and God*, pp. 368-9).

This I Ask in Jesus' Name

I once wrote a book on the healing miracles in the Gospels — reflecting on the stories of those who were healed, and at least one disciple, Paul, who was healed in spirit but had to go on in faith carrying his "thorn in the flesh" with him. I have participated in a number of healing services. I have seen people made whole and also shared in the lives of those who were not healed. I have prayed for and seen the power of God's love and have meditated on the mystery of suffering and pain and a Savior who was crucified.

Here is the story of one of Jesus' disciples, a woman whose faith and courage are a witness to me. With her permission I share it with you. Her words are addressed directly to her Lord.

Lord Jesus,
David in the Psalms cried out to you in his anguish. He cried out in his fears, his doubts. He asked for deliverance from persecution and from distress. I, like David, cry out to You now. Hear the voice of my cry as I sing this Psalm to you.

I hear from my sisters, brothers and friends of Yours, that Your love is so deep for me, You desire to heal me. I hear that You want to take this mangled body of mine and reassemble it.

They say, Lord, that You love me so much — that You do not want any of Your children to be in "bondage." Lord, they showed me all of the miracles that you performed; the miracle of the Loaves and Fishes, the time that You healed the blind man and raised Lazarus from the dead.

Lord, a sister took me to my first of many healing services, a Kathryn Kuhlman meeting at the Shrine Auditorium. She said that the Holy Spirit told her that she was to take me to that particular meeting, and that I would be healed. "My faith isn't strong enough," I told my friend. This sister whom I loved with all of my heart, and felt was anointed by You, wanting to see me "whole" said, "Joanne, you don't have to have the faith; remember the paralytic man who had to be lowered through the ceiling of a house? Christ healed him — not because of his faith, but because of the faith of his friends." Lord I did remember that! "My faith will get you healed today," she blurted out. I was so frightened for her and wondered what would happen to her faith if I wasn't healed. I wasn't healed that day!

When I was younger, I looked at my disabilities as a blessing from You, Lord. I saw it as an opportunity to reach out to others in real love; to show them that even with a messed-up body, one's heart doesn't have to be messed-up. I often used my disability to make people laugh. I felt, Lord, that You made me with a special handicap, one not so severe that it would hinder me from functioning, yet severe enough to keep me humble and dependent upon You. Five years had passed since my Kathryn Kuhlman experience, the questions began as my relationship with You grew!

I read, Father, in Psalm 139 where David writes that "You formed my inward parts, You weaved me while I was still in our mother's womb. I am fearfully and wonderfully made." Paul also writes in 1st Corinthians that You chose the weak things (people) in the world to shame the things which are strong. I felt Your love and plan for my life in these passages.

Now I am feeling so many doubts. I'm wanting to be healed, but I do not see it in Your plan for me. Lord, is it selfish of me to even want such a thing? I know so many others who are in need of Your healing more than I. Please Lord, make known Your will to me.

I am involved with a beautiful group of Christians, whose love toward You and me are great, and who are into this "healing business." We study about Your Son's healing powers. We learned that Jesus healed every single person who same to Him to be touched. He healed Peter's mother-in-law sick with a fever; a deaf mute who didn't even know You. He healed a woman who had been suffering from a hemorrhage for twelve years and all who were demon-possessed. The marvelous thing that I learned was that You used these miraculous miracles just to bring others to Yourself!

Anyway Lord, as I was saying... after studying some more about Your love for others through the use of this gift, my friends, and more importantly I, wanted to be touched. "If I could only touch the hem of Your garment, I too will be healed," I thought. I really started believing, Lord! The more we prayed, the more we saw visions of my back straightened and my hands being steady. I believed that any day, any moment, You were going to heal me! My faith was stronger than ever. I watched miracle after miracle being called out on television by Oral Roberts and yes, Kathryn Kuhlman, and knew that any time they would be calling out mine. Little children were rising from their wheelchairs and walking for the first time. Drug addicts and men and women with all kinds of infirmities were being healed. I knew that You wanted that for me also, but they never called mine out! A minister told me that when I received my healing, what a testimony I would be for others. "Joanne, when people look at your life, they will see what Jesus has done and you will bring glory to Him." *I could* see that and believed You wanted that also.

I no longer saw how I could be used in my present condition to enhance Your kingdom. I was being turned down for jobs such as working with disabled children, sharing my understanding and compassion with them. I was missing out, Lord, on meaningful relationships with men because of the physical qualities on the outside which I seemed to lack. The desire for that healing grew greater.

I no longer wanted to use a typewriter to write a simple note to a friend or to accept a drink in fear of spilling it all over or even go through the embarrassment of writing out a check with a line full impatient people looking on. I just wanted to feel free to lift up my hands in praise to You and to be able to stand in a group of people to tell others about Your love, power and grace.

I thought that my healing was coming through a type of brain surgery, but the doctors decided that it would be too risky. So, I knew that my miracle would just have to come straight from You. I woke each morning, Lord, looking for my healing, testing first my hands and then my speech. Looking and waiting for something that never came.

My friends continue to pray for me, for which I am deeply thankful. As for me, sweet Lord, I have simply given up! Forgive me, Lord. Please be patient. Show me more about Your healing grace and where it fits into the scheme of things for my life. Remember this poem that I wrote called "Tomorrow"?

> *I know that tomorrow will be brighter,*
> *My joys will be many, my trials will be lighter —*
> *I know I'll experience a real healing,*
> *My limbs will be perfect; it will be quite thrilling.*
> *I'll run to my friends, be able to shout,*
> *Look at me precious ones, see what Jesus is about.*
> *He took me all mangled and broken,*
> *He mended me, loved me; He cleansed me from all sin.*
> *He showed me His Son and His death on the tree.*
> *He shows me how with His Spirit I'm free.*
> *Tomorrow will be such a happy day.*
> *For You are the potter, Lord; I am Your clay.*

Jesus, thank You for being my potter! I don't know if You choose to heal me tomorrow when I wake to a new morning or tomorrow when I come into Your heavenly kingdom. I am trusting in You for my answers.

Share with me, teach me Your will, mold me into the person that You want me to be. If You choose to heal me right now, give me the faith to believe it. And, Jesus, if You will it, that I remain just as I am... use me and all of my limitations for Your glory.

This I ask in Jesus' Name. Amen!

This Worldly Bible

When I was yet a young man, and before I had begun my theological studies, I was taught a basic understanding about the Bible: The Bible is in the world as Jesus was in the world. This analogy, I learned, was fundamental to a faithful biblical theology.

The Catechism of our *Book of Common Prayer* states the catholic view this way: Scriptures are called "the Word of God because God inspired their human authors and because God still speaks to us through the Bible."

Much of my ministry of teaching and scholarship in seminaries and universities, and now as bishop, has been concerned with helping people hear and experience how a compilation of books written and put together a long time ago can inspire, guide and help us understand our lives today.

One of my concerns has been to reflect on the vital and necessary interaction of Scripture, tradition and reason that enables the Bible to be our guide and become the "architecture" of our living faith. Scripture has a primacy in this interplay while tradition and reason have vital and essential roles. We are called to be wise and enlightened as we develop our understandings.

Our reasoning, while it should do its best to encompass the whole range of human knowing, must also recognize human fallibility, and being reasonable, now our capacity for rationalization and self-centeredness.

In the Anglican tradition of Christian living much reasoning wisdom comes from pastoral experience. Well it should, because one can regularly see Jesus dealing with persons and situations in pastoral ways.

Jesus is heard upholding the ideals of marriage. He spoke against remarriage after divorce. He taught in the circumstances of his own time when it was possible for husbands, following the word of Moses in the

Hebrew Scriptures, to divorce their wives for little cause and to leave them in precarious and defenseless situations.

Christians must continue to hear these words seriously and to reckon with the difficult pastoral consequences of divorce. But many have also come to believe there can be a creative Christian response when the intention for a life-long marriage can no longer be fulfilled.

The Bible is in the world as Jesus was in the world. The Bible itself tells us that Jesus had to be made like us in every respect (Hebrews 2:17). He could not be our Savior unless he had experienced all human limitation. Part of human limitation is not to be able to see into the future or fully understand the past — certainly not to know everything about every subject. Jesus was part of his own culture and time.

The wonder of God's saving love is that it comes to us in real life — in and through our limitations. And it is in these worldly and changing circumstances that we hear stories from the Bible that are often about struggle — between order and chaos, freedom and slavery, justice and injustice, life and death. Amid suffering and uncertainty, the stories tell of hope and the victories of the power of God's righteousness and love, especially in the resurrection of Jesus. Above all, the Bible is about the character of God's love and concern for God's people penetrating into an often inchoate and broken world. It is about God's hope for the kind of people we may become.

The moving power of these stories, and the hope and faith engendered by them, motivate and guide the people of God. It is that overall guidance which empowers communities of worship and faith today. However people of the biblical worldview may at times seem to have tolerated racism, slavery or accepted a lesser status for women, we together hear a calling faithfully to insist that racism, sexism and slavery cannot be a part of a church or community in which all are recognized as being made in the image of God, and there is to be "neither Jew nor Greek, neither slave nor free, neither male nor female; for you are all one in Christ Jesus" (Galatians 3:28). It is the same moving power to love and for true community which calls us faithfully to work out in living, pastoral circumstances what it means when our church claims that gay and lesbian people are full members of this Body of Christ.

The Bible is in the world as Jesus was in the world. Often, when people were searching for answers they would ask Jesus a question: "How often should my brother or my sister sin against me and I forgive them?" "What must I do to inherit eternal life?" "Why do you eat with tax collectors and sinners?" "Who is my neighbor?" Or "Bid my brother divide the inheritance with me."

Jesus responded with a story — sometimes telling of both judgment and extraordinary love and mercy at once. "What you are most searching for," he seemed to say, "is not some simple answer to your question — not just a few words. You hope to discover what really matters — what is of true value."

The stories of the Bible become catalysts for our own stories of forgiveness and grace, of courage and hope. Together these stories lead to the experience of God's ways for human life — what Jesus called the kingdom or ruling ways of God. Although there are many contemporary matters the Bible does not address directly, still today, we believe, this is what the Bible leads us toward: God's ways, God's love, God's Spirit — known best to us through Jesus — in our lives. Is this not what we most long and hope for?

Sharing in Korea

A n American of my age cannot be in Korea without remembering the Korean War. It was then that I first heard of places like Pusan, Inchon, the Yalu River, and a battle site called Porkchop Hill. Had I been but two years older, I might have fought in that war. I had friends who did and one who died. So I cannot help but think of all Korea has gone through in this extraordinary century — its long and sometimes harsh occupation by Japan, the bitter three-year Korean War, and the dividing of its land between the Republic of South Korea and Communist North Korea. While we were in Korea in October of 1996, tensions had again been heightened between the South and North by the infiltration of a group of North Koreans by means of a small submarine.

This history and hardship makes all the more remarkable the economic and social development which has taken place in South Korea during the last forty years — lifting the standard of living of the great majority of the population and transforming the landscape around its urban centers — particularly the city of Seoul which, until recent changes in governmental policy, experienced a great influx of new population. Indeed, many recognize that one of the greater challenges the country now faces is that of controlling environmental damage while continuing economic development.

Knowledge of the Christian faith did not come to this historical land of Shamanism, Buddhism and Confucianism until late in the eighteenth century, and, because of persecution and fear of outside influences, it did not take root until well into the next century. Christianity then, however, began to grow, and now more than thirty percent of the population has become Christian of one denomination or another — a far greater percentage than is to be found in any other Asian country.

Together with Barbara and Joon Matsumura, now serving as a bishop's liaison with the Asian congregations, I had been invited to Korea by the bishops of the three dioceses of the Sung Koe Hoe (Holy Catholic Church), the Anglican Church of Korea, and most particularly by the Bishop of Taejon, Paul Yoon, who from 1982 to 1987 had been vicar of our Korean congregation in Anaheim. The invitation included the opportunity to visit the church in Taejon and Seoul and to offer lectures to the clergy and at two of the universities.

The Anglican mission to Korea began in the 1880s when individual missionaries from China and then the Church Missionary Society from England began active work. In 1889, the Rev. Charles Corfe, formerly a Royal Naval Chaplain, was consecrated at Westminster Abbey, and later celebrated his first eucharist in Korea on Christmas Day, 1890.

The Anglican Church shared in the turbulence and many of the hardships of Korea in the succeeding years. Bishop Cooper and several of the clergy, along with sisters of the Holy Cross, were taken into captivity during the Korea War. Sister Clara died of hunger and beatings, and one of the clergy died because of the cold. The Anglican Church continues as a relatively small church in Korea known, along with other missionary churches here, for its strong support of education. It also is recognized for ministries with the poor and disadvantaged. In 1993, the Sung Koe Hoe became an independent province within the Anglican Communion.

After a twelve-hour flight, we arrived at Kimpo International Airport late on a Tuesday afternoon. We were kindly met and driven to our hotel in Seoul where we unpacked and tried to sort out the changes to our watches and biological clocks (flying entirely during daylight, we had "saved" seven hours coming to Korea but were now actually seventeen hours ahead of Los Angeles time because of having crossed the International Dateline). We soon gave up and went to bed.

Early the next day we were driven to the small town of Chopyong where the Diocese of Taejon has a new church building. (Bishop Yoon, who has training as an architect, helped design the church.) To the clergy and spouses and friends of the diocese, I there gave the first of my lectures on the healing stories of Jesus. Professor Peter Kim had generously translated it into Korean which made it possible for many to follow along without too much additional translation. I was gratified to see how the clergy of the diocese came together with such good spirits and to find a number of younger clergy who are intent on continuing their education.

We proceeded on to Taejon, the growing sea city of 1.2 million people. The next day we had breakfast with the governor of the province and met with the mayor of the city before going to Hannam University, an educational institution founded by Presbyterians, for the second set of lectures. This was followed by a luncheon with the president of the University and various Anglican faculty.

Throughout our trip we were met with extraordinary hospitality and a graciousness for which the people of Korea are known. The exchange of gifts (the centennial of our Diocese of Los Angeles was thus taken to Korea) was an important part of a number of occasions and the meals were memorable — probably remembered on my waistline as well as by my hamstrings as I learned to eat, especially in the Taejon area, sitting on floor mats in traditional Korean style. I rate my skill with chopsticks at about B-minus. Barbara says it's more like a D. The hospitality even extended to our efforts to pronounce a few expressions of thanks, greeting and farewell in Korean. It also makes one remember how hard many Korean-born people have worked to learn English.

Later that afternoon, we visited the Social Welfare Center and the House of Sharing — service ministries to the elderly, youngsters, handicapped persons and people seeking a new start in life and re-employment. These are largely government-funded and led by dedicated priests of the diocese. We were moved and quite taken with these ministries.

The next day we were able to visit the ancient Popchusa Buddhist Temple in the Songnisan National Park where it is thought that at one time there were as many as 30,000 monks in residence. It was an overcast, rainy day, but the mists in the mountains graced a particularly lovely part of Korea. The following day we returned to Seoul where on Sunday I preached to two services in the newly completed and impressive Anglican cathedral in downtown Seoul. We were treated to lunch with vestry members, and I was able to meet with the mother and a brother and sister of Jonathan Won, rector of our St. Francis Church in Norwalk. We had in Taejon earlier been well hosted for dinner by Martin (another of

Jonathan's brothers) and Veronica Won. While in Seoul, I was also able to talk with the Rev. Benedict Koh, the brother of Aidan Koh, now also ordained, who assists at St. James' Parish, Wilshire Boulevard, and is chaplain of the school there.

Our last two days in Seoul involved a visit to another House of Sharing ministry in the Seoul diocese, a tour of the Korean Folk Village and a lecture at the Song Kong Hoe University, an Anglican institution. Our host there was the president, the Rev. Dr. Jae Joung Lee, whom I had earlier come to know on a trip of his to Los Angeles. He and I also had opportunity to talk about planning for the Lambeth Conference where I hope his understanding of cultural and Christian diversity will be a help to the Section of the Conference entitled "Called to be a Faithful Church in a Plural World."

On our last evening in Korea, we enjoyed a dinner with Bishops Yoon and Matthew Chung of Seoul and Pun D. Kim of Pusan and Mrs. Chung, a last gracious challenge for the waistline and chopsticks.

Among some of the good questions I was asked after the lectures, two now stand out. One came from the clergy of Taejon who knew of large churches in Korea which seemed to offer a Christian faith that promised blessings of health, happiness and even financial success to believers. Was this a faithful presentation for followers of Jesus? The second question, in many ways similar, came from the Christian president of Hannam University who asked if Christianity in Korea might not have become too closely linked with a kind of capitalistic theology and perhaps partly, as a result, a Christianity not showing sufficient care for the unfortunate in life.

We talked then about how Jesus' healings were first of all signs showing that even those most set aside by society because of various handicaps were invited into God's reign of mercy, rightness and peace. We reflected on Jesus' way of compassion which called, like the prophets before him, for special care for the less advantaged. We remembered Paul's "thorn in the flesh" and the challenges he, and many after him, had discovered in trying to follow the way of Jesus.

We did not answer all our questions about the character of God's blessings, Jesus' healing love and the way of the cross, but I was reminded how these matters — in both similar and different ways — are also challenges for the church and for disciples in the United States.

Just before leaving for Korea, I had worshipped with, and shared lunch with, members of our St. Nicholas' Korean-American Church, part of our larger Cathedral Center congregation, and I had met with our Korean-American clergy. I look forward to doing so again and also meeting once more with the people of St. Francis' in Norwalk, for I have gained much through hospitality, conversation, and friendship in Christ with a church some seventeen hours ahead of us. I have learned about ways we can become more involved in mission and ministry together. As soon as I get my biological clock reset, I want to share some of that.

On the Death of
Matthew Shepard

We are met here before this federal building in a great and terrible sadness — in tears because a young man was tortured and murdered. We weep because a life full of hope and promise — that of a 21-year-old fluent in Arabic and German — was so cruelly ended; his skull fractured, his body burned and beaten, and left — here in our United States — in thirty-degree weather tied to a fence, his arms extended, all too reminiscent of a crucifixion. Who among us does not weep?

We weep for his parents and family, for his friends and classmates. We must weep as well for four other young people — so terribly, terribly misguided, their lives now in ruins. We weep this day, too, for the twenty or so other men and women who were killed in our society last year, and the year before that, and the year before that, because of their sexual orientation.

How in the name of God can we stop this? What in the name of God brings on such brutality?

Not all the time, but sometimes, it is in the name of God that such prejudice is loosed and persecution may seem to be sanctioned. That must not, must not be. Matthew was a member of the Episcopal Church, a member of my church, a member of the Canterbury Club on his university campus. Still more importantly, he was a child of God — the God of all life — the God who cares for and seeks to redeem all life.

I hope that the four young adults who had a hand in torturing and murdering Matthew did not have some warped ideas about religion in their heads. But we know they could have. I know that several kinds of religious leaders and politicians, holding that they represent certain religions or religious-cultural view points, have condemned this killing. Yet we must also be clear in our understanding how readily language about purported deviancy and sinfulness seeps into our culture and becomes the additional fuel of cultural prejudice and hatred for those who, in their own insecurities, think they cannot deal with differences.

I believe, as my church affirms, that gay and lesbian persons are all "children of God." They have "a full and equal claim with all other persons upon the love, acceptance and pastoral concern and care of the Church." They, too, are part of our family values in the fullest sense, for they are often our brothers, sisters, our nephews and nieces, our aunts and uncles, our parents and children. They are fully, as Matthew was, part of the body of Christ, and we pray, by God's grace, still are members of the communion of saints — those whom God has made and loves as they are made — sexual beings, whose sexuality, I believe, also can become fully human through commitment, caring and sacrificial, vulnerable love. It is self-giving love, and mercy, justice and compassion that the bible is finally about. What I hope and pray the Christian faith — all religious faith — is all about.

And right along with this faith — and in any event — I belong to a church, and I hope a society, which at the least insists that homosexual persons "are entitled to equal protection under the laws with all other citizens." Surely this should and must mean protection from all hate crimes.

Forty of our states already have forms of such laws. These laws do not, as some might have us believe, prohibit any freedom of religious speech. Wyoming, however, has no such law, and now we need laws for us all that will apply to all of our society, that will reach into every mind and, we pray, into all hearts as well: insisting, demanding that hatred against any group of persons, against human beings, children of God, and any such brutality, the murder of a young man like Matthew Shepard, ought not — must not — again happen among us.

One More Death Can Bring No Closure

One's heart continues to go out to the families and friends in Oklahoma City who lost those so precious to them in the Murrah Federal Building blast. If anyone does not deserve to live, that man is their murderer, Timothy McVeigh. No manner of protest from those opposed to the death penalty is going to change his sentence.

His death, however, will not — because it cannot — compensate for his crimes. Sad to say, it is psychological jargon to suggest that his execution will bring "closure" for anyone. Nor can we claim that his being put to death will help prevent more murderers, any more than the threat of capital punishment deterred him. To the contrary, the spectacle of it all may make our society another notch more brutal. Another government-sponsored killing may give a bit more license to the next troubled teenager or other person who feels he, too, has just cause to kill.

No matter how much we might wish it otherwise, the moral order cannot be changed. Violence cannot be redressed with another violent act. "The ultimate weakness of violence," Martin Luther King Jr. reminded us, "is that it is a descending spiral — begetting the very thing it seeks to destroy. Instead of diminishing evil, it multiplies it. Through violence you may murder the liar, but you cannot murder the lie or establish the truth. Through violence you murder the hater, but you do not murder hate.... Returning violence for violence multiplies violence, adding deeper darkness to a night already devoid of stars. Darkness cannot drive out darkness; only light can do that. Hate cannot drive out hate; only love can do that."

The father of Julie Welch, a young woman who died in that dreadful explosion, makes the same point. "The execution of Timothy McVeigh will not bring back Julie or her colleagues, nor will it end the grieving for any one of the victims.... Revenge and hate are the reasons 168 people died that day in 1995. I oppose the death penalty absolutely, in all cases, because in all cases it is an act of revenge and hatred."

The warden of the prison where Timothy McVeigh is to be executed tells us that he will be put to death "professionally" as the sun comes up that morning. I am far from sure how professional we can be about injecting poison into another living person and standing by until he can no longer breathe. I am far from certain that our morning will become any brighter or that we will have accomplished anything at all for our humanity.

We have every right to do all we can to protect people from Timothy McVeigh or any future Timothy McVeighs. But Dr. King had it right. Only good can overcome evil. When we have awakened to our sunrise and coffee after his execution, we will feel no better or wiser or satisfied for what has been done on our behalf until we vow to do all we can to prevent further crazy violence by people thinking they are going to find revenge. Although it may seem ironic, one small step in that path will be no longer to license the vengeance of the death penalty.

Mothers in Prison,
Children in Crisis

We the people have put Sandra in prison because she has a drug addiction. Her husband and the father of her kids can't be found; and six-year-old Taran and four-year-old Sarah have been taken in by Sandra's mother, who is trying to cope with them and her own deteriorating health. She may soon have to give them up to foster care.

Taran and Sarah haven't seen their mother in more than six months. She is sick with her concern for them. They are bewildered and do not understand what is happening. They are, for all intents and purposes, orphans. Both of them are showing signs of emotional and psychological disturbance. Statistically they are becoming likely candidates in years to come to have deep-seated problems of their own.

It costs society $25,000 a year to keep Sandra in prison — to which we may soon add the costs of foster care for Taran and Sarah. So add another $30,000 to the bill. It also costs over $100,000 just to build the prison facility for Sandra.

Another woman named Jacquie also has two children about the ages of Taran and Sarah. She was found guilty of the same drug-related offenses that put Sandra in prison. Her problems were, however, dealt with by a drug court and her sentence was a strict program of counseling and drug treatment with community service. She and her children are being given health care, and she has received job development and employment assistance along with help in finding child care for the children. The cost for these programs and assistance for Jacquie and her children is under $5,000.

You and I are left scratching our heads and weighing our hearts. How did we develop a system where there are so many more Sandras with Taran and Sarah than Jacquies with her children? And there are at least ten times more of them since 1980 — many because of non-violent addiction related offenses.

What lack of political will and courage, of common sense, of family values, of caring for children and mothers, of fiscal sanity led us to this? What mental and spiritual laziness? For, yes, it is a kind of laziness that would just shut mothers away in prison rather than going about the tougher community work of treatment and counseling, and job and child-care assistance.

Jacquie and her children are not out of the woods. There are problems ahead — an abusive husband who may return, and some work-related instability on her part. The kids, however, are doing much better, and she is trying hard to be the best mother she can be.

For God's sake let us help her and many like her to have a life — and not a prison. For God's sake let us help their children have their mothers.

The Holy Scriptures of Judaism and Christianity, indeed, of all religions, tell the people of faith that they are to have a special care for those who society would otherwise push aside — not least the children. We are to care for the orphans — not make orphans. We are to have care for families — for poor mothers. We are to help build up and to restore. For God's sake, and our own, let us advocate and work together to give children to their mothers and mothers to their children.

September 12, 2001:
Durban, South Africa

First of all, let me thank you for being here this morning to pray and weep with us and to share your concern and compassion for all the tragedy, suffering and death in the United States. Barbara and I are far from home.

Being able to be together with you means a great deal to us. As many of the people of our church and country prayed and cared for you during the viciousness of apartheid, we now crave your prayers and love as we seek to heal and to halt the circle of violence and terrorism in our world.

In so many ways we are aware again that we do live in a global village where what happens in one part affects many others. For Barbara and myself, our first concern was our son Matthew whose offices are close to the former towers of the World Trade Center. He saw the second plane crash and had some horrific experiences, but we are greatly relieved to learn that he is alive. We were able to reach him by telephone late last night, and also to learn that his fiancée, who was on a plane from New York to San Francisco, is stranded but safe in St. Louis. We are so grateful to Bishop Rubin and Rosemary for the tenderness with which they took us in and the love and prayers we shared last evening.

Next, we had to be particularly concerned with the people on the three planes that were bound for Los Angeles. But our hearts go out to everyone involved, not least the fire and policemen who died trying to save others. We pray for all who died at the Pentagon. The dying and all the bereavement are beyond words, and for a few moments I ask you to be silent and in prayer with me.

Several of you have told me that you have fears for relatives of yours working in the financial district of New York. I am sure that a number of people from England and Europe, from Asia and the Middle East, too, and other lands, had come to work that morning and fearfully died. Such dreadful terrorism does not care about human suffering. It is blind to the terror and death it brings to individual human beings. In the terrorists' obsession with their cause, with revenge and getting even, with putting an end to what they have demonized, they can focus on monumental buildings and people whose humanity they no longer share. Their inhumanity blinds them to the fragility of other humans who bleed and die. They refuse to see moms and dads, children, the orphaned and weeping children, the brothers and sisters, the tears for a lifetime.

In too many places and in too many times there is a ring of violence in human life and history. Revenge and violence are sanctioned to try to murder wrongs or somehow to even things out, but the hatred and violence circle back again. Martin Luther King had the moral law right when he insisted that "the ultimate weakness of violence is that it is a descending spiral — begetting the very thing it seeks to destroy."

The United States and all those countries whose people were killed have the right and responsibility to do what must be done to capture or stop those whose hands are bloody. Some measure of good may come as peoples around the world come together to do this.

I also have questions to ask about the morality of an international financial system that allows an Osama bin Laden, whether or not he was involved in this monstrosity, to harbor and spend his two or three hundred million dollars for death and terror. What we must not do is join the terrorists in the vengeful or "collateral" killing of innocent moms and dads, children, brothers and sisters.

Somehow, we must instead join in trying to prevent violence in Palestine and Israel, all the sickness of so many children in Iraq, the millions of deaths in Congo, wherever violence continues to pursue the ring of violence and violence's repression. We must, above all, pray and recommit ourselves to work for world peace.

You know too much about violence and violent repression in South Africa. In challenging circumstances you are working hard to build a new country based on forgiveness, and reconciliation without revenge, and I know how many of you also long for world peace and are willing to try to be the peacemakers, doing the prayer, the forgiveness, the sharing and reconciliation that make for peace in our world.

Last week, a Conference Against Racism and, indeed, against violence and all repression, was held in this city. I regret that the United States of America was not a leading participant in being sorry for the evil of slavery and its consequences wherever it has taken place.

I want us to take the lead in being against racism in all its forms at home and abroad. If we believed that some misused the Conference and the media for a message lacking in reconciliation, we could object and dissent that part of the Conference, but let us, unafraid in the future, at least join in, if not take the lead in being against racism, hatred and repression at home and abroad in all its forms. As Desmond Tutu, in his typical way, said after the Conference, too many people forgot the delegates were supposed to be talking about people whose tummies were hurting.

Conferences, however, come and go. Stopping the ring of violence and putting an end to terrorism take far more commitment and deeds as well as words of understanding of others, of fairness and peace. For the moment in my country, there is much shock and many tears. We, along with other families in the world, must bury and deeply mourn our dead. We are to do all we can to put an end to terrorism without wreaking more violence on the innocent flesh and blood of our world.

Out of our agony we must resolve to be the reconcilers and workers for peace. It is night now at home, but soon it will be morning. You can be sure that the spirit of the United States will strongly revive, but let us pray that as it does so it will, before all, be a spirit seeking the genuine peace we believe God wants for all God's people.

Thank you again for being with us. Thank you for joining your prayers and tears and compassion with our own. We shall bring them home with us and share them with all your brothers and sisters and ours.

Kind and Generous in the World

This is a defining time in United States history. Our President has described us as a kind and generous people victimized by a senseless and vengeful atrocity. This gives us a right and duty to respond to what has happened and to try to prevent any such future terrorism.

The use of violence to end violence will always run the grave risk of escalating violence. This we know from world history and from our own recent actions and those of others in the Middle East. New martyrs are forged, and angers grow hot and sometimes explode in worse violence. Martin Luther King often reminded us that violence is a descending spiral: "Returning violence for violence multiplies violence, adding deeper darkness to a night already devoid of stars. Darkness cannot drive out darkness, only light can do that. Hate cannot drive out hate, only love can do that." To have any chance of reducing future violence, the response of the United States to the terror at the World Trade Center and Pentagon must be done in the name of justice and be carefully focused to as to avoid more suffering deaths of the innocent.

However complex and difficult it may be politically, we will do best to continue to develop a consensus of peoples and governments and to act within that framework, strengthening rather than weakening the United Nations as we do so.

Whatever the military response, there is still time, and it will be far more significant in the longer view to think about our response as a kind and generous people. A sense that the United States is a caring and generous country, trying to make better lives for all people in the world, would do more to show up the bleak negativism of terror and violence and to isolate its sources than all our military might and measures ever could or will.

However generous and kind Americans may be as individuals, shown by many in the aftermath of September 11, we must yet recognize that this is not the perception of how we act collectively as a government in the world. Even our friends are shocked by how little we share with others through foreign aid and the United Nations. While many billions of dollars flow back to the United States as the biggest seller of weapons to the developing world, fewer billions of dollars could make an enormous difference in alleviating the effects of world poverty and the unnecessary deaths of hundreds of millions of children from disease and malnutrition. To many our only response seems to be lectures about the virtues of free trade and American-style capitalism and free enterprise with little recognition of the historical and economic forces that make any form of catch-up in a competitive world economy difficult without our assistance and willingness to be sure that trade is not tilted in our favor.

The wide disparity of have and have-not countries continues to grow rather than lessen. Meanwhile we walk out of or away from conferences and agreements that are mean to confront problems of racism, children's rights, and the environment when we do not think they suit our interests. Others are left with the impression of a unilateralism and even arrogance. We will not even stay participants and argue our own case if we do not think we can win our way.

Many people still admire and look up to the United States, but kind and generous would probably not be the first words to come to mind to define our collective actions and attitudes toward the developing and often troubled parts of the world. Think what it could do to the sources and resources of terrorism if many of the world's people saw the ingenuity and generosity of the United States making us the leader, through the United Nations and in other ways, in respecting the dignity of all other human beings by doing much more to alleviate poverty, disease and lack of human opportunity.

Christians are meant to believe that a violent death on a cross has been transfigured by a love that is to be shared with others. There are those, I am sure, who will regard a call to generosity and kindness as a naive response to terrorism, but there is abundant evidence that a hope violence can do the work of ending violence is the ultimate naiveté. If we are truly to honor our dead, we can best do so by gifts of life rather than more death. If we are ever to transform the terrible pictures of exploding planes and collapsing buildings into anything other than symbols of terror and death, Christians and Americans of other faiths and no religion will need to join together with the same Spirit to help inspire the leadership that will enact our kindness and generosity in the world.

Hymn for Healing

The chaplain at our Good Samaritan Hospital, David Walker, asked if I would write the words for a hymn relating to health care and its ministries. He noted that even though we have many hospitals and, of course, doctors, nurses and others who work in healthcare — along with so many of us who have been or will be patients — there are no hymns for this important part of life.

I was intrigued with the opportunity and awareness that the words I would write would be set to music by David, who is such a distinguished musician and the composer in our Hymnal of *Point Loma* for "Baptized in water, sealed by the Spirit" and *General Seminary* for George Herbert's "King of glory, King of peace."

Here is our hymn.

Hymn for Healing

In - fi - nite in all di - rec-tions, Are the won - drous worlds in worlds,
When our liv - ing is in bal-ance, Bod - y, mind and spir - it tuned,
Some - times it will be a strang-er, Whom a - lone we can be - friend,
For in time our need will be there, To re-ceive the love and care,
With our lives, we pray, in bal-ance, Bod - y, mind and spir - it tuned,

Vast be - yond all com - pre - hen-sion, Hid - den in the at - om's swirls.
Work and pleas - ure joined in cad - ence, Harm - o - ny is well as - sumed.
Touched with care in spite of dan - ger, Like the good sam - ar - i - tan.
Call - ing on the wound - ed heal - er, In a dark - er hour of prayer.
Work and pleas - ure joined in cad - ence Harm - o - ny now well, re - sumed,

In - tri - cate in each di - men-sion, Love's in - tent with - in the strife,
May we know your Spir - it's pre-sence, In our health when flour - ish - ing,
Nurs - es, doc - tors, ev - 'ry work - er, Ther - a - pist and coun - sel - or,
Then a - gain our faith is grate-ful, For your Spir - it's strength-en - ing,
We will praise for the cre - a - tion, All that's known and mys - ter - ies,

Form and cha - os so in ten - sion, Lur - ing thought and faith to life.
Well our strength then used in ser - vice, Tend - ing oth - ers' suf - fer - ing.
Each to - geth - er as the neigh - bor Help the oth - er's health re - store,
For the heal - ing arts so skill - ful And each heart for us car - ing.
Off - er - ing our life's ob - la - tion, For your ways of love and peace.

Words: Frederick Houk Borsch, 1996
Music: *Good Samaritan Hospital*, David Charles Walker, 1996

♩ = 66

8.7.8.7

❖   3   ❖

Jesus Is Here
and
Other Ministries

Jesus Is Here

The four-year-old had tugged the door open and now stared at me. I knew Billy from the Sunday school class at the church where I was the curate. I had come calling to see if I could visit with his parents. Wide-eyed and without turning his head, Billy shouted to his mother, "Mom, Jesus is here!"

I heard a kind of indistinct sound (a sigh or exclamation of surprise), and Billy's mother, a bit flustered and disheveled, came around the corner from the kitchen where she had been engaged in some chore. Billy gave my leg a hug, and his mother and I chuckled in a slightly embarrassed way before we sat down to talk about church and family matters.

Later I thought of her reaction in that moment after Billy's announcement and before she got to the door. She must have heard those passages from the Bible about the Lord's sudden return. "You do not know when the master of the house will come, in the evening, or ar midnight, or at cockcrow, or at dawn."

I laughed to myself again. I find that a number of clergy have had something like this happen. There is, after all, all the talk about Jesus from us, often when we are dressed in special clothes. It is no wonder that some children become a little confused about who is who.

Nor is that the end of it. Because we are ordained and in special roles in the life of the church, we are right in suspecting that more than a few of the people of God expect us in some special way to represent Jesus, to be in some ways like Jesus.

We want to protest, but perhaps still to have it a bit of both ways. Few of us are above wanting to be thought at least a little special, but "Hey, I'm not Jesus." In any case, we all know laity more devout, more self-giving, in these ways more like Jesus than we are.

Yet we also know that everyone of us is called to grow "to maturity, to the measure of the full stature of Christ." We are to be "ambassadors of Christ" and so to represent God's reconciling and passionate love in Jesus to others. All Christians are called to do this, but certainly not least those who have been authorized to be stewards of the sacraments and to preach the good news.

I have stood in that doorway many times since in my life, knowing full well my foibles and frailties, along with Paul's awareness that "we have this treasure in earthen vessels," but also thinking of Desmond Tutu reminding that we carry Jesus' reputation in our hands as well as those awesome words of Teresa of Avila:

> *Christ has no body now on earth but yours; no hands but yours, no feet but yours; yours are the eyes through which is to look out Christ's compassion to the world; yours are the feet with which he is to go about doing good, and yours are the hands with which he is to bless us now.*

Just a Few Words

During the last ten years I have probably tried to get too much mileage out of telling the story of how I was six-foot-three-inches tall when I began this ministry, but that there have been so many occasions when those who introduced me to speak have whispered, "Bishop, please be short," that this is how I have come to my present five foot seven.

Often, however, there can be virtue in a few words. Sometimes they could become mere slogans, but at their best they sum up and point to whole areas of life and ministry. As we have together in this region built up our churches and built new ones and have gone through challenges and opportunities for service amid drought, floods and fires, severe recession and economic dislocation, immigration and demographic change, the world's costliest earthquake, civil upheaval, poverty for many in the wealthiest of societies, the tragedy of our criminal justice system, bizarre murders and trials, dealing with our own clergy misconduct and church differences, I have found myself returning again to a few basic themes to help guide us and lead us positively forward in mission.

Thank you for choosing me to be your bishop. I thank each of you for your ministries and my great staff and clergy colleagues. Thanks to God for these challenges and opportunities to seek with you to go forward in faith as disciples of the Lord Jesus. Thankfulness is the pulse of our spirituality. In gratitude, I will have a gift to share with each of you when we come together in the weeks and the year ahead.

Adelante is to me a poetic word which sounds something like what it means. Forward together. It is a welcoming and inviting word which can speak across languages, suggestive of the ethnic richness, past and present, of our region. It is a word which calls us to the first of the three major themes of our mission statement: to be a *welcoming people*, an *inviting people*, a *Pentecost people*.

We recall the first pentecost story when the gospel message spoke directly to people of different backgrounds and languages. So in this most diverse region the world has ever known do we have the opportunity to share in the life of God's Spirit in welcome, faith and service with those of different races, ethnicities, orientations, ages.

Education. We can do this more effectively by knowing and understanding our faith as mature Christians called "to the measure of the stature of the fullness of Christ," growing in head knowledge and in heart knowledge in wisdom.

Young People. With them we are called to a ministry with the children and youth in our churches, neighborhoods and communities. We are to nurture them, befriend them, listen to them, teach them, help develop their ministries. If they are among the poor and disadvantaged in our society, we are to reach out to them, seek to strengthen their families, offer our support, sometimes adopt them, vote on their behalf, advocate for their education, safety and health. What other would God have us do for all God's children?!

In all these ways do we build up our faith communities and congregations as *power stations for the Holy Spirit*. In these ways do we discover that we *all have ministries* to which we are called at our baptisms. In the words I have used to commission all those renewing their baptismal vows at our Easter celebrations, we are to be *ambassadors for Christ*, God making the appeal of reconciling love through us.

A number of these themes have become part of our mission statement. When I recently volunteered to take that statement and see if I could make it more concise and also to see, as I rather boldly advertised, "if I could make it sing," it also occurred to me (it is so obvious, isn't it?) that it ought to be a prayer, too. And I commend that idea to all of you who have mission statements for your churches, institutions or programs.

But, several of you, however, then challenged me, "But we can't sing it yet." Now we can.

MISSION HYMN
OF THE DIOCESE OF LOS ANGELES

1 One in prayer and in our wor - ship called to jus - tice, love and
2 As God's pen - te - cos - tal peo - ple, giv - ing thanks and of - fering
3 Build - ing ser - vice con - gre - ga - tions, min - is - tries with all our

1 U - no en or - a - ción y cul - to, lla - ma - dos a a - mor y
2 Pue - blo de Dios pen - te - cost - al, da gra - cias y al - a - ban -
3 Min - is - te - rios ju - ve - ni - les, i - gle - sias pa - ra ser -

peace, the dis - ci - ples of Lord Je - sus we would
praise, we will share faith's in - vi - ta - tion with those
youth, be-com - ing wise and en - light - ened, A - de -

paz, los dis - cí - pu - los de Cris - to ser - vi -
za, in - vi - ta - ción de fe da - mos a to -
vir, sa - bios en la luz de Di - os, A - de -

serve God with - out cease. Come,_____ Ho - ly Spi - rit, come.
born in all life's ways. Come,_____ Ho - ly Spi - rit, come.
lan - te! in God's truth; Come,_____ Ho - ly Spi - rit, come.

re - mos sin ce - sar. Ven,_____ Espí - ritu San - to, ven.
da crea - ción de Dios. Ven,_____ Espí - ritu San - to, ven.
lan - te en su ver - dad; Ven,_____ Espí - ritu San - to, ven.

Phrase 1 of each stanza may be sung by one group, with a contrasted group singing phrase 2, and all joining for the final phrase.

Words: Frederick H. Borsch (b. 1935); tr. Carmen B. Guerrero (b. 1941)
Music: *Bridegroom*, Peter Cutts (b. 1937)

♩=90

87. 87. 6

Who My Dog
Thinks I Am

'God, please make me the person my dog thinks I am." I saw that bumper sticker the other day. I laughed, and when I came home, I looked in Sydney's eyes. Sure enough; I was the greatest guy in the world! Although it was late in the day, I had come home just in time to play with him. I patted him and rubbed his tummy. He licked my ear. I threw the ball for him and gave him his dinner. I was a kind, fun-loving and generous person who loved my neighbor as myself. Certainly, I loved Sydney.

A dog, we say, is a best friend — seemingly always ready to forgive our being late, understanding, ready to play and give a sticky lick, never expecting us to be mean or uncaring.

At their best, I realized, that is what all friends are for: perhaps not the sticky lick, but the understanding and forgiveness and, above all, their hopes for the best of us. Our best friends hope that we will be good and generous persons, not always thinking of ourselves, not mean or selfish, but caring for others in our lives.

That is especially true of the good parent, too. I know my mother has always expected that of me, even though she has seen my faults pretty clearly as well.

Years ago, there was a youngster living on our block who I had a hard time believing anyone could love. He seemed to be always dirty with a runny nose and a precociously sarcastic mouth. Several times I admonished him for kicking gravel from my driveway on to the lawn. Once I saw him push a little girl off her tricycle.

Then one day his parents invited us over for dinner. As we were sitting in the living room with our chips and wine, down the stairs came the boy. He had just had his bath and was in his blue and white pajamas. He climbed on to his mother's lap. She kissed him and ran her fingers through his shining hair.

Martin Luther noted that the human tendency is to live our lives *incurvatus in se*; that is, curved in on ourselves. In the more colloquial version of it, people wrapped up in themselves make pretty small packages. The calling of our loved ones is to uncurve and unwrap us — to forgive us and to love us so that in knowing ourselves to be loveable we can become *loveable*, able to love.

Jesus said that we are to be friends and that there is no greater love than to give one's life for one's friends. Jesus not only spoke of this, he showed us the self-giving and offering way of God's love.

Because of this friendship and love, Jesus also has great hopes and expectations for the best in us. "God with God's all-merciful eyes," wrote the author of *The Cloud of Unknowing*, "sees not only who we are and have been, but who we will be."

God puts great faith in us and who we can be as God's people. Blessed are the humble in spirit who do not put themselves first in life. Blessed are the merciful and those who hunger and thirst for righteousness, fairer and more just living. Blessed are the pure in heart. Blessed are the reconcilers and peacemakers, for they will be called children of God.

So, Sydney and Mom and my friends and Jesus, help make me and us all the persons you believe and hope us to be.

You Don't Say

"That meant so much to me, what you said about angels cooling us with their wings." Did I say that? Every preacher has been surprised by what people have taken unto themselves from a sermon compared to what was thought to have been said. It is a humbling experience to have crafted a sermon in which the main points were one thing and someone then thanks you for having said another thing. The Spirit of God seemed to have used one's thoughts and words to bring something rather different to this individual.

Perhaps it more often happens with the use of an illustration or story. Along the way the story may remind hearers of something that once happened to them or something they thought or heard on another occasion. The preacher, however, is thanked for having brought it up.

Such gratitude is a little easier to deal with when the sermon was some time ago. I have had people tell me how much they appreciated what I said in a sermon more the fifteen years ago. I have trouble remembering the occasion, much less what I preached about. As they go on I cannot even imagine that I would have said that in the way. Maybe it was someone who looked like me or a preacher named Bork instead of Borsch. Or perhaps, again, what I had said brought another message to them.

It's a bit tougher, however, when one has just delivered the sermon and someone gives thanks for words you are certain you did not utter. The first temptation may be to give them a little shake and try to explain again what you failed to get across. Yet they seem so glad and grateful for what has been given, one doesn't want to take that away.

At times, of course, it can go the other way round, with the hearer offended or hurt by something the preacher did not intend. As a pastor I have learned to listen attentively at moments like these, for the Spirit may have spoken to the person in his or her own pain or confusion or need. There may yet be an opportunity to make the misunderstanding an occasion for new understanding and grace. I have a friend who to this day thanks me for saying something in a sermon which made him quite angry at the time. I do not think I could now ever convince him that this was not what I said.

My most humbling story of God using a preacher for other than the preacher's intended purpose may not have involved words at all — at least not many of them. During the first year or so after my ordination, there was an elderly Welsh woman in the parish where I was curate. Lucy was in her early nineties but spry and still sharp. After each of my fledgling sermons she would tell me of her appreciation. My estimation of her intelligence and perceptiveness continued to grow. "Father Borsch," she would say (I was all of twenty-five, but this was in the Diocese of Chicago some years ago), "I just do not know how you continue to put together such fine sermons."

One Sunday Lucy came up to me after church with her kind smile. My heart rose as I readied to hear her wise approval. "Father Borsch," she said, "you were so good and helpful this morning. But," she paused with a wince of consternation in her eyes, "my hearing aid wasn't working, and I couldn't hear a word of it."

It took a moment before it dawned on me that Lucy must mostly have liked how I looked in the pulpit or my vestments or the way I flapped my arms. Or maybe she was just one of those gracious souls given to us for encouragement and support.

Maybe, however, there was a little more to it. Perhaps occasionally a few words of my sermon had gotten through and that was all she needed to make her own sermon and hear God's word to her. By God's grace it may be what happens more often than we know.

Clergy Anxiety Dreams

You cannot find your sermon notes or you have lost your place. You cannot find the right page in the prayer book or the Bible. You cannot find your vestments or are dressed in the wrong ones. The dream seems to go on endlessly. Darn! On and on! You are probably tossing and turning. It becomes a nightmare. You mumble something and break out in a cold sweat. You are relieved to wake up and slowly figure out it was a dream. You laugh a little nervously to yourself. "Why did I have that dream again?"

Every profession, I am sure, has its versions. Other clergy I have commiserated and chuckled with confirm those three major categories of clerical anxious dreaming. You have just lost your notes, your place in the service or your vestments. And, there is always enough that happens in life to fuel such dreams. Years ago, I was invited to preach in a large English church where there were probably less than a hundred people present. During the opening hymn, however, some two hundred young men marched in and filled all the side aisle seats. When I nervously inquired of the vicar, I was told they were "borstal boys" — lads from the local juvenile home.

Mumbling under my breath, I began to reconfigure my sermon, trying desperately to think of something that would speak to the young men. All too quickly the collect, lessons and psalm flew by, followed by the gradual hymn and the gospel. What was I going to say? I wasn't yet sure how I would begin. Then, during the hymn before the sermon, all the borstal boys filed out again. I was left with the original congregation.

I remember a cathedral dean solemnly pronouncing: "the first lesson is from the Book of Habakkuk" and then muttering "darn Habakkuk, darn Habakkuk!" as he leafed through the large lectern Bible trying to locate the prophet. Sitting there I recalled the times I could not find the right reading or collect or proper preface.

In real life God is still praised, and every liturgy, thank God, does have an end. But one does not know that in the dream which is a part of its high anxiety.

The other night I found myself in one of our churches and had forgotten to bring the proper vestments. Nor did they seem to have any right ones. Colors and sizes were wrong. Try this, Try that. Suddenly I was in my underwear. Then they gave me a pair of pants which were way too large. I could not go out there like that! Off went the alarm.

Whew!

Dwellers, Seekers, Practitioners

Robert Wuthnow is a sociologist of religion, a researcher, commentator and interpreter of culture, of faith and religious practice. In his book *After Heaven: Spirituality in America Since the 1950s*, he looks back over changing sensibilities and practices. Many Americans, he suggests, passed from a dwelling-oriented sense of their religion and spirituality to a seekers-orientation. The former is based in an imagery of dwellings and habitat in more settled communities and institutions. The now familiar imagery for the seekers is that of the journey.

While life can be said to need both dwelling and seeking (roots and wings), many people have found during recent decades that faith was no longer what they inherited, but that for which they had to strive. They were passing from a time of stability in bricks and mortar to the information age. Communities were no longer stable. People experienced themselves as part of temporary groups that formed and subsided. More choices were available, including the options of other religions or aspects of other religions. Eclecticism was one of the options, and some of the more popular spiritual and psychological writers became deft at such blending on the road to greater self-discovery and finally on to so-called new age religion. Wuthnow archly comments: "...the road less traveled is, as pundits note, a veritable four-lane highway of book buyers, retreatgoers and spiritual seekers. The reason is perhaps, as historian Lawrence Moore has observed, that the way to be 'in' in U.S. religion has always been to pose as an outsider..." Following psychologist James Hillman, Moore uses the phrase "psychological polytheism" to "capture the kind of self that has many different claims made on it and is able to find small truths in many places..."

A host of hyphenated self-words characterized the seeker-orientation: self-acceptance, self-emancipation, self-esteem, self-fulfillment, self-identity, self-realization and, perhaps most importantly, self-expression. The fluidity of life (in marriage and family, information availability, acquaintance with other religions, occupations, people moving about) all were part of a growing uneasiness about objective knowledge itself. With the loss of a sense of habitat came an emphasis on freedom, living without rules and a stress on personal experience. Wuthnow quotes the psychologist Carl Rogers: "Neither the Bible nor the prophets — neither Freud nor research — neither revelations of God nor man can take precedence over my own direct experience."

Into this emphasis on personal experience fit therapy for some along with the healing of past experiences and addictive behaviors. AA and other twelve-step and recovery groups helped many and were a means of self-improvement, also providing at least a form of community and sometimes also spirituality.

Much of this analysis is, of course, at the level of generalization and runs the risks of simplification. It is also true that this book seems largely concerned with middle-class white folk and would need a broader interview base to be fully descriptive of spirituality in the United States. That being said, the study is yet full of well observed reflections, and Wuthnow intersperses his commentary with quotations and bits of the life stories from the people interviewed. They speak of the benefits of their journeying and seeking, although there is often a note of something missing — of perhaps some longing for the past or an imagined past of spirituality that has been lost in the "privacy" of contemporary spirituality. One hears comments like "my spirituality is in shreds" and "my beliefs are darkened and cobwebby" which accompany the loss of a sense of habitat and transcendence.

There also has been considerable criticism of much of this journeying and seeking as being facile and requiring little of its followers (conformist in their ways?) in terms of responsibility, discipline, sacrifice and service to others. In particular, the lack of community experience and its involvements is often critiqued.

While there is no going back to the habitats of the past, Wuthnow does see some shifting taking place — more awareness of the significance of community and the development of what he describes as practice-oriented spirituality. Although there still is a tension between religious institutionalism and spiritual practices, this sensitivity is caught in a quote from a woman who says, "No matter how imperfect the organizational church is, we need it. We need community; sure, I pray alone... but I also need community."

What Wuthnow discerns and also commends is more than just an emphasis on techniques of prayer and spirituality. Nor has practice-oriented spirituality lost all aspects of the seeker-mentality. But, with a greater community dimension, has also come, he believes, a greater sense of the need for discipline and involvement. At the heart of it is a willingness to practice, and, one hopes, to try to practice spirituality in all aspects of life. In his last paragraph, Wuthnow observes that "Traditionally, the spiritual ideal has been to live a consistent, fully integrated life of piety, such that one's practice of spirituality becomes indistinguishable from the rest of one's life. The Benedictine David Steindl-Rast expresses this view when he writes, 'We must avoid putting too much emphasis on practices, which are a means to an end. The end is practice, our whole life as practice.'"

One may add that the best spirituality — of a living faith — has always had its community, seeker and practicing dimensions. We may pray and strive to see that this is what our churches offer people today.

Neighborly Notes

I imagine that many of you keep clippings and scraps of reflections from here and there — from someone's newsletter, a quotation jotted from a book, a talk you once heard. Martin Marty must be the master at this. I'm afraid that I am far less organized. I do have a 3" x 5" card file I keep some quotations in, but then I cannot think what to file a particular idea under. Others never get transferred to the cards. Instead they pile up on top of the file or are put in already bulging folders.

The advantage of this lack of system is that quotations from different times and places can arrive in interesting juxtapositions. I found three such today as I was ruminating post-Lambeth Conference — thinking of the things I want to share and about all the hope I have for life and ministry together.

First from Sam Laeuchli, who in his book *The Serpent and the Dove*, held that "there is an infinite gap between orthodoxy as dynamic search for authentic response and orthodoxy as an established formula."

Then the end of a sermon from the great Desmond Tutu:

> Let us go forth, then, as the followers of this Jesus, ready to celebrate life that can't be lived by rote. Let's luxuriate in its complexities, in its bewildering ambiguities, excited by the thrill of working out things for ourselves. Let us celebrate our diversity opposing the new xenophobia that is abroad, knocking down the walls that would keep the stranger out. Let us go forth ready to be surprised by a God who gives us some strange fellow workers — just look at the archbishop of Cape Town! — to be ready to cooperate with such a God as we work to follow his set of pri-

orities to make our community, our society, our world more caring, more gentle, more compassionate — that we won't just pass by on the other side those sleeping on the rough, the homeless, the drug addicts. We will be like the students I met recently in Oxford who care for children with disabilities in a project called KEEN, or those who work with the Sisters of the Community of All Saints in the project Porch, or what is done in this very church, communicating the love and compassion of God. Let us go forth and embrace and love and care for those whom some want to turn into lepers, people living with AIDS. Let ours be inclusive communities, welcoming and embracing, refusing to exclude people on the basis of culture, ethnicity, faith, gender, or sexual orientation. Go forth to celebrate that we are indeed the rainbow people of God.

And finally this paraphrase of Romans 8:18-25:

It appears to me that whatever we suffer now will show up only dimly when compared to the wonders God has in store for us. It is as though all creation is standing on tiptoe longing to see an unforgettable vision, the children of God being born into wholeness.

Although creation is unfinished, still in the process of being born, it carries within a secret hope. And the hope is this: A day will come when we will be rescued from the pain of our limitation and incompleteness and be given our share in a freedom that can only belong to the children of God.

At the present moment all creation is struggling as though in the pangs of childbirth. And that struggling creation includes even those of us who have has a taste of the spirit. We peer into the future with our limited vision, unable to see all that we are destined to be, yet believing because of a hope we carry so deep within.

First Ride

Nervy words of confidence and questions,
replaced now by twitchy silence,
watching my wrench
turn the nuts. I pull the bolts, and safety
of the training wheels falls away.

Cinch no longer, it will not even stand
without a hand. I give to his,
watching the eyes,
as he holds mine in trust that I will let
him go, but not until he says,

and tries alone to make the wobbling straight,
crying not, and without laughter
should he falling
hard on the skinning sidewalk or, we hope,
softer grass, need support again.

Calling for release, he yet lurches left,
then back into me heavily,
so sweet a weight
I could hang on, recalling my blue bike,
and with it my dad's strength and smell

late one afternoon, when I feel them both,
letting touch go, seeking balance,
as I do cry
and cheer us on when he begins to ride,
thinking perhaps he's on his own.

Day-by-Day

I received a letter recently from one of our clergy and asked for permission to share it.

Dear Fred,

I'm sure most clergy could make a list like this one, but it struck me funny, being as it ran from the sublime to the ridiculous, and I thought you might like to see it. This is what I did on the first week back from vacation, in no particular order.

With the music team, planned music for five Sundays, including the Bishop's visit, and the Blessing of the Animals on Saturday, October 4.

Attended meetings of the Ecclesiastical Court, the Program Group on Mission, and Deanery Council.

Wrote and pasted up parish newsletter.

Counseled a church member who had discovered that her son was addicted to cocaine.

Provided spiritual direction for a directee.

Wrote two sermons, one in Spanish.

Said Mass at St. Mary's Convent, brought parishioner along. Stayed for breakfast.

Learned that a parishioner I had spent three months get-

ting into the Episcopal Home was behaving inappropriately and would have to leave. Contacted his sister to come from Kansas, arranged for her to stay in my guest house.

Met with and prayed with a homeless family several times (they are members) and told them they could no longer park their motor home in front of the church, run an extension cord across the sidewalk and plug into the church's electricity.

Met with Bishop's Warden, planned agenda for Bishop's Committee, and developed a strategy for putting church's accounts on computer.

Met with CPE students from local hospital with their Chaplain. Led reflection on their hospital experience.

Set up meeting to assess the future of the Spanish service.

Asked two members to organize brunch for Bishop's visit: one "no," one "yes."

Four meetings, consultations about the inappropriate behavior of two youth on campout.

Met with Deanery Committee about transferring workshops from "New Ways of Doing Ministry When the Money's Tight" to the Ministry Fair.

Met for contemplation with Centering Prayer group, coffee afterward.

Met with Sexton, developed list of tasks to be done by volunteers while he is on three-week vacation.

Led mid-week healing and Eucharist service.
Telephoned and talked with two shut-ins.

Presided and preached at three Sunday services.

Arranged for next meeting of clergy support group. Called everybody.

Conferred with chairman about details of Blessing of the Animals.

With Spanish teacher corrected and practiced Spanish sermon.

Formally asked a member to head the Altar Guild. She said yes.

Re-wrote two contracts for our after-school theater workshop for at-risk youth. Met with them separately re start-up tasks and payment schedules.

Wrote job description for a third staff position, arranged to advertise the position, set interview date.

Took three children to lunch.

From John Coburn I first heard the observation that so much of our ministry takes place during the interruptions — while we are making plans for our day or week or life. It does not mean we cannot or should not plan, but it does mean there will be a lot else going on.

I did visit with that priest and congregation a few weeks ago and joined in celebrating all the mundane, incarnate, everyday, tiring, hopeful, courageous, sublime and ridiculous parts of our lives and ministries.

Wiggle Your Toes

You are about to chair an important meeting. A quiver of nervousness rides up your back. Or the gradual hymn is coming to its last stanza. You would so like this sermon to go well. Eyes will soon turn your way. Have you prepared enough? A ring of panic begins to constrict your throat.

Wiggle your toes! This was the best piece of advice ever given me for moments like these.

For one thing, no one can see what you are doing inside your shoes. It may not be much, but you are getting away with something no one else knows about.

The activity gives you another thing to feel for a moment, and it is relaxing in itself. The rest of your body can sense those toes wiggling.

Kids wiggle their toes, barefoot on a summer beach, or with their legs dangling from a parent's lap. And it's not bad to feel the child in you — to gain a little perspective on one's whole self and on the significance of what is to take place.

You are God's child, too. Your worth and being loved is not dependent on present performance. Indeed, it is for others that you are doing the best that you can.

No, you may not have time to think all these thoughts while you are wiggling your toes, but enough of them. You are ready to begin.

Apt Teachers

While the character and responsibilities of the ministry of "over-seers" (*episkopoi*) or bishops were still in a formative stage during the New Testament period, one can already see and understand the significance of the teaching role. Among the attributes and virtues of a bishop as set forth in I Timothy 3:2 is the ability to be an "apt" or "a good teacher." We can rightly imagine that the Greek word *didaktikos* carried suggestions regarding disciples who not only knew the basic faith in order to pass it on, but who were also sufficiently skilled as speakers or rhetoricians and as interpreters of the Christian message into the circumstances of the people so that the faith was presented persuasively. The word occurs again in the context of advice to Timothy "not to be quarrelsome but kindly to everyone, an apt teacher, patient, correcting opponents with gentleness" (II Timothy 2:24-5). In the letter to Titus, no doubt in a time when there was a growing awareness of ways in which the basic faith message could be distorted, the bishops' teaching role is seen as more protective. They are to have "a firm grasp of the word that is trustworthy in accordance with the teaching" (*didache*) so that they "may be able both to preach sound doctrine and to refute those who contradict it."

At the heart of all Christian teaching and, so especially for those who were leaders in proclaiming the faith, was the resurrection of Jesus. To this they were to be witnesses or *martures*, a Greek word soon to carry a sense of those willing to suffer and even die for their faith. When Matthias is chosen to take the place of the ministry and apostleship from which Judas "turned aside," it is said that he "must become as witness with us to Jesus' resurrection" (Acts 2:22). Paul's summary of that which "I handed on to you as of first importance" of what "I in turn had received" begins with

Christ's dying for our sins in accordance with the scriptures and then tells of the resurrection, of which Paul is himself, though as "one untimely born," also a witness (I Corinthians 15:3-11).

From the list of virtues which occur in the Pastoral Epistles of I and II Timothy and Titus and in a passage like I Peter 5:2-3, it is also evident that those who carry forward the teaching of the faith are to witness by their lives as well as their words. The elders (or presbyters) who are to tend the flock of Christ are to do so by exercising the oversight (*episkopountes*) not under compulsion, but willingly, as God would have you do it — not for sordid gain but eagerly. "Do not lord it over those in your charge, but be examples to the flock."

Here is an important note we shall want to reflect on in subsequent contexts: the teaching role cannot be described as separate from all else the leader does. The words and the service and ministry must go together.

Early Christian teachers no doubt often remembered that Jesus was regularly addressed as rabbi or teacher in the Gospels and clearly saw himself called to teach. As good teachers must do, he taught in a variety of ways, using different kinds of stories and sayings to tell how God's reign could already be begun even amid human wrong and suffering. Vital in the first disciples' re-tellings was their recollection that Jesus had said as he had done. He not only told of reaching out to the lost, he had done so — to Bartimaeus and Zacchaeus, to Mary Magdalene, the man with the many demons, and to the foreign lady whose daughter was demon possessed. He not only had spoken the Word of God, he had enacted it. Later Origen would describe Jesus as *autobasileia* — the one who had embodied the kingdom about which he taught. And finally, and most powerfully, this enactment was made known in his passion, death and resurrection. Commissioned by Matthew 28:19 and the power of the Spirit which comes upon them to make themselves witnesses (Acts 1:8), disciples are to go forth and themselves tell the stories of and about Jesus. No subsequent teacher could do all that Jesus had done, but none were or are meant to forget or forego his example. In their own ways they, too, are to teach by word and deed.

One image for the fullness of this ministry found in I Peter and again in Acts 20:29, is that of feeding the flock — feeding the people of God.

This is a sacramental ministry. It is a pastoral ministry. But it is also and always a ministry of teaching. Both in I Peter 5:1-3 and also in the Acts passage (see 20:17 and 28) we hear how fluid the descriptions of leadership roles still were with elders sharing in "oversight" or "episcopal" ministry. Even though in but a few generations this episcopal ministry took on more specific definition, it will be important for us later to remember that *episkope* was and is always a ministry of the whole Church.

In this sense as well, the work of teaching and witnessing are always together the work of the Church. Some are called to particular roles as leader teachers, but, as we hear at the examination at the ordination of priests, "...all baptized people are called to make Christ known as Savior and Lord." The ministries of presbyters and bishops are to be understood as helping the whole Church to do this ministry.

The word *episkopos*, which had only a general meaning in Greek usage, gained its more particular definition through Christian experience and usage. Augustine would look into the root meaning of *skopos* and stress its sense of intention, to intend, to direct intention, and hence of *episkopos*, to superintend, and, with specific reference to the ministry of teaching, to see that the faith is correctly taught.[1] In this work, the bishop was a steward — one who preserved the faith but who did so by making good present day use of it. The tension inherent in preserving by making good use of the faith is a recurrent theme in the ministry of bishops as teachers and theologians.

The second and third Christian centuries saw a growing emphasis on the place of bishops as personal symbols of unity and continuity in the life of the Christian communities. Ignatius and Hippolytus gave primacy to the bishop's unifying role as presider at the Eucharist.[2] Irenaeus, keenly aware of the need for faithful and forceful teaching in order to contradict false understandings and interpretations, spoke of bishops as having received the apostles' place and teaching for this ministry.[3]

The major occasions for the bishop to teach were at the Sunday liturgy where he regularly presided and as the principle catechist for those preparing for baptism.[4] "In both the East and the West in the patristic period," the 1990 Report of the Archbishop's Group on the Episcopate notes, "the bishop was theologian and homilist, expounding scripture and put-

ting the faith into words for his people. In the best of such leadership —
exemplified in the West in Ambrose, Augustine of Hippo, Gregory the
Great — spiritual discernment, intellectual powers and sound judgment
went together."[5] Beginning with Ignatius, Irenaeus and Athanasius, that
list, as Charles Price points out, can be extended in our own tradition to
include, among others, Cranmer, Jewel, Temple, Michael Ramsey, William
White, John Henry Hobart, Charles Henry Brent, Edward Lamb Parsons
and Angus Dun.[6] And to this some of us might add, again among many
others, Lancelot Andrewes, and, in our own century, Ian Ramsay, John
Moorman, Stephen Bayne, John Krumm, Desmond Tutu, Richard
Harries, Stephen Sykes, Arthur Vogel and, not without controversy, John
Robinson, James Pike and John Spong.

As, however, the Church expanded in metropolitan areas and grew to
envelop whole countries, bishops often found themselves with larger dioceses and could no longer be in regular contact with their people, certainly not on a Sunday-by-Sunday basis or as the primary catechist for those
to be baptized. Much of this teaching, and the theological reflection to
accompany it, would come to be done by other clergy and lay leaders. Yet,
while bishops had to share this ministry, they continued to have a central
and leading role — the bishop, in the language of the Episcopal Church's
Study Document on the Ministry of Bishops, being described as an
"anchor person" in the Church's entire teaching ministry.

In the Concordat, which may soon bring full communion and
exchange of ministries to the Episcopal and Evangelical Lutheran
Churches, both Churches "agree that a ministry of *episkope* is necessary
to witness to, promote and safeguard the unity and apostolicity of the
church, and its continuity in doctrine and mission across time and
space..."[7] More broadly through the World Council of Churches, Lima
Report of 1982, the important document "Baptism, Eucharist and
Ministry" speaks of the place of bishops in the ecumenical ministry as serving "the apostolicity and unity of the Church's teaching, worship and
sacramental life." [8]

Much of what we have observed to this point is summed up in a resolution of the 1982 General Convention called "Principles of Unity"
which is a reaffirmation of the "Chicago-Lambeth Quadrilateral." In its

explication of the fourth article dealing with the historic episcopate, the resolution holds that:

> Apostolicity is evidenced in continuity with the teaching, the ministry and the mission of the apostles. Apostolic teaching must, under the guidance of the Holy Spirit, be founded on the Holy Scriptures, and the ancient fathers and creeds, making its proclamation of Jesus Christ and the Gospel for each new age consistent with these sources, not merely reproducing them in a transmission of verbal identity. Apostolic ministry exists to promote, safeguard and serve apostolic teaching. All Christians are called to this ministry by their baptism... We understand the historic episcopate as central to this apostolic ministry... Bishops in apostolic succession are, therefore, the focus and personal symbols of this inheritance and mission as they preach and teach the Gospel and summon the people of God to their mission of worship and service.[9]

This teaching role finds liturgical form in the rite for the Ordination of a Bishop (*The Book of Common Prayer*, pp. 512-523) as the new bishop is "called to be one with the apostles in proclaiming Christ's resurrection and interpreting the Gospel, and to testify to Christ's sovereignty..." This work of proclaiming, interpreting and testifying is to be done in a number of ways, not least by seeking to be "an effective example in word and action, in love and patience, and in holiness of life,"including the showing of "compassion to poor and strangers" and defending "those who have no helper." In order to carry out this ministry the new bishop promises "to be faithful in prayers, and in the study of Holy Scripture" in order that he or she "may have the mind of Christ." As the newly ordained bishop is handed the Bible he or she is asked to "Feed the flock of Christ,"...to "guard and defend them in his truth, and be a faithful steward of his holy Word and Sacraments." A high point in the liturgy comes when this successor to the apostles, "chosen to be a guardian of the Church's faith," is asked to lead the people in the confessing of that basic faith in the words of the Nicene Creed: "We believe..."

II

Two of the questions directed to new bishops at their ordination ask "Will you guard the faith, unity and discipline of the Church?" and "Will you boldly proclaim and interpret the Gospel of Christ, enlightening the minds and stirring up the conscience of your people?" Perhaps in every generation, but likely in some times more than others, bishops will feel the tension between those promises to, on the one hand, *guard*, and, on the other, *boldly proclaim* and *interpret*. One could, indeed, maintain that every bishop ought to experience the tension intimately — that it is of the gospel faith to do so.

In important ways a living faith is always changing. The expressions of that faith not only may but should continually be renewed and renewing. In his book *A People Called*, Paul Hanson helps us to see again how the religion of the people Israel was constantly changing, from that, for instance, of a more nomadic to a more settled people, from less to more cultic forms, with and without a temple, in times of prophets and of wisdom teachers, in times of exile and return, of war and peace.[10] What was constant in all this change was a faith in and the worship of the God of both insistent justice and great mercy — a God of holiness calling the people to holiness.

That which was critical, in other words, was worship (praise — *doxa*) of the right, true and only God (orthodoxy) and not worship of something less, as the people are always tempted to do.

It was this faith that Jesus proclaimed and enacted in his conviction that the realm of God's holiness was already begun even amid life's sin and suffering. The disciples' renewed faith in that realm, together with their faith in Jesus and what God had done in him, is the story of hope and salvation. The basic story is told by many voices. The hesitancy in the early church to put the story into writing probably had much more to do with the desire to preserve that tradition of living witnesses and voices than any difficulties in finding individuals capable of producing that record.[11]

As it came to be written, it found a variety of forms, expressive of the different experiences of the faith in the several Christian communities. This can be seen not only in the four (and, at first, more) gospels, but in the letters of Paul and other early Christian writings. While one can hear the same core story, the church to whom the Epistle to the Hebrews was written was clearly different in many ways from the church from which the

Gospel of Mark emerged, as were those of the Gospel of Matthew and the Gospel of John. In the disagreements between Paul and Peter and the matters one can discern being discussed and sometimes settled regarding, for example, christology in the fourth Gospel and church discipline in Matthew's Gospel, the desire for certain measures of conformity in the interpretation of the faith can be seen. More remarkable, however, is the apparent openness to variation. While this could be explained by the lack of means to shape and enforce such conformity during that period, it would seem to have had much more to do with the character of the basic faith and the need to interpret the core story into differing circumstances. Particularly in the writings of Paul, it is evident that what is vital is centered in the faith in God's reconciling activity in Jesus and not the establishment of a new uniform religion.

Yet soon, in the Pastoral Epistles and elsewhere, one can see the pressures calling for more uniformity in interpretation and practice. They come from a natural and positive need as time went on to have continuity and identity in the telling, interpretation and expression of the faith, and also to indicate that certain attempts at the interpretation of the faith were in some ways aberrant — to combat "heresies" which did not sufficiently or rightly express and interpret the central faith. The stream might be broad, but there were shores, for otherwise the waters might flood and the direction and character of the river be lost.

Now, however, the tensions inherent in both preserving and sharing and interpreting the faith were more fully met. Should not the river sometimes flood the land about it? Sometimes a river needs new channels. Were and are there not dangers, too, in making banks too steep and narrow?

What is necessary for the identity and continuity of the faith? Is it only the basic "story" — incorporating the essential stories — of the faith? By whom then and how then are those stories selected? And story by its very nature calls for interpretation. What measure of like interpretation needs to be attached to the story of faith for there to be an identifiable people of the same faith?

Let us ask a fundamental question by way of illustration. What happens if the understanding that God is the creative source of all life is lost or in some way mitigated?

We might agree that teachings about God as the creator and source of all life are essential in the understanding of the story of biblical faith, but let us now make our case more difficult. Is a teaching of *creatio ex nihilo* also one of these essentials? Over many centuries and still by many theologians it is held to be an essential — necessary to the understanding that all things are dependent upon God and that God and God's being are not part of or dependent upon anything apart from God. A host of theologians and even official church pronouncements have welcomed the so-called big-bang theory in contemporary physics (as opposed to a steady-state theory) as being compatible with the traditional *creatio ex nihilo* understanding.[12]

Yet there are theologians, perhaps particularly process theologians, who have thought of a *creatio continua* or some sense of God bringing form and life from the chaotic as being more in keeping with the opening words of the Bible and the cruciform shape of the universe. Or it may be that the reality is more profound than any teaching can yet properly imagine — even that *creatio ex nihilo* and a *creatio continua* are somehow complementary rather than antithetical.

But is not some form of *creatio ex nihilo* still an essential tenet of the faith? Many would hold that it is, arguing that anything less could mean that there were aspects of creation which are not of God.

What then of people who do not hold to it?

What should be done about them, especially if they are in authoritative teaching positions? Never apart from questions about faith, essentials are questions about people. Issues about essentials in belief and practice in every religion (along with other forms of community) can often boil down to who is in and who is out. Powerful in the reminiscences of the disciples is Jesus' inclusion of many — both in his teaching and in his actions. His radical teaching offered the invitation to God's realm to all. God's forgiveness and accepting love, enacted by Jesus, come first, even before repentance. Forgiveness and acceptance enabled repentance. A firm grasp on this understanding undergirds Presiding Bishop Browning's prophetic teaching that there are to be no outcasts in this Church.

Yet, if the invitation is unconditional, what happens if the invitation is refused or largely neglected or wrongly understood? Did not Jesus also teach that the way was narrow and demanding of response? Cannot people in some ways cast themselves out? Are there no boundaries? Can people say or do whatever they want and call it Christian? What does it mean to be a follower of Jesus Christ?

Or, let us put the questions and the tension in a somewhat different form. It is well-known that definitive forms of Christian interpretation and teaching were shaped in the first Christian centuries in a hellenized culture. While we are rightly warned not to make too much of a hebraic versus hellenistic dichotomy, it is fair to say that the evangelical and apologetic efforts of Christianity in a hellenized context strongly influenced much Christian understanding. How definitive and lasting should that shaping be? Is it, as part of the work of the Holy Spirit in history, essential to Christian teaching and interpretation today? Or does that hellenistic influenced theology itself need to be interpreted or even largely discarded so that a fresh interpretation of the basic story can be made? This is a matter not only for those living in "post-hellenistic" western cultures, but for those living in Asian and African cultures which were never directly influenced by hellenistic thought.

The *pentecost* story tells of many peoples hearing the mighty words of God each of them in their own native language. One might understand that evangelistic activity only in terms of the translation of words, but even the word *only* begs the question. How does one translate atonement and reconciliation and, for that matter, forgiveness and love from one language to another when languages themselves are so bound with culture?

In other terms, distinction is often made between content and form — the essentials of the faith and the ways they are expressed. The distinction is not without value, but form and content are not always easy to separate. Indeed, at that very point will often come the tension.

If all this were only a matter for detached theological reflection it would be one thing, but in efforts to share the gospel faith in different times and cultures the issues become very practical and pastoral. It is all too easy, for example, as we all now know, for one culture to assume that its ways of expression and understanding are the ways. So may a local culture or local theology establish itself as a kind of universal theology.[13]

Examples from the history of Anglican colonization and evangelism are too numerous to mention, but I particularly enjoy the story of what was said to have happened when an elderly English bishop stood up at the 1978 Lambeth Conference and asked, "What holds the Anglican Communion together? We used to have a common prayer book, a common language, a common sense of ordination. Now there are all these different liturgies, so many languages, and some churches are ordaining women. What holds us together?" he again asked plaintively.

After a pause, lengthy enough to let the question hang, an African bishop spoke up and answered, "Wippell's."

That Wippell's is an ecclesiastical haberdasher in many parts of the Anglican Communion all too well illustrates the issues inherent in the English bishop's question. To put them in a more formal sense we may ask, even if it were a matter of some ease to decide what are the essentials of the faith, (what is the *esse* of Christianity), are there still not matters of what is attached to that *esse* which many would regard as important to the fullness (the *plene esse*, as it is sometimes called) or the valuable (the *bene esse*) of the Church's life?

The bishop was asking what gives the Church its identity. How do we recognize it? How do we know we are members of one Church?

My purpose here, however, is not to try to answer the many questions we have raised so much as to illustrate them and the importance of recognizing the inherent tensions involved in both guarding and boldly proclaiming and interpreting the faith. The Report of the House of Bishops' 1967 Advisory Committee chaired by Stephen Bayne reminds that faithfulness to God in the search for truth "plainly requires of the community the ceaseless, arduous way of relating his saving acts in the gospel and the Church to all else he does."[14] The Report goes on to point out that seeking to do this in times when people tend to be suspicious of authorities and questioning, whether there is any lasting knowledge or truth only makes matters more complex. It then continues:

> Every generation, we suppose, looks back on its predecessors with envy, coveting for itself the supposed certainty which the earlier people enjoyed. But there are few more deceptive reflections than this. The tradition of the Church, its continuity, is always, in every generation, a matter of constant disturbance. One need

only recall the vehement debate as to Christ's nature ... or reflect on the contemporary controversy about just or "limited" war, to be aware of the ceaseless anguish through which the Church's tradition is received and transmitted.[15]

We have reflected here, in other words, on reminders that evangelical and apologetic work on behalf of the faith is always challenging and worthy of our best thought and attention — with bishops among our leaders, but on the part of the whole Church. It is important because this is what the Church is to do. One cannot just conserve the faith if one is to share it. If it is to be carried forward, and so conserved, it has also to be liberated from interpretations which may disguise (as may an overlay of political or patriotic ideology) or fail to communicate its essentials. This involves more than repetition, more than translation in any simple manner. In a more technical sense, it involves hermeneutics — not just translation and interpretation, but thinking about how that is best done. It involves probing and exploration, for to do less would not be faithful to what has been given. "The spirit of theological inquiry," as John Courtney Murray put it, "is immanent in the very dynamism of Christian faith itself."[16]

This may involve disturbance, for there cannot always be full agreement about what is essential and what not, nor what is of the *plene esse* and *bene esse* — about the best ways of interpretation and how they affect the essentials. And that brings back to mind the charge to "boldly proclaim and interpret." There ought always to be something bold about the faith's proclamation. Orthodoxy has always been bold. Insisting that God was not just a leading god among many was bold, as was insisting that God was fully present in the fully human life of Jesus was bold. Nor has ferment always been bad for the Church. Sometimes it is just that which helps make room for the Holy Spirit. In some of these times of ferment the Church has grown vigorously.

Yet, if it is good to risk on the side of boldness, when and how might boldness overstep its bounds? Let us look for a few moments at a rather well-reported time in the life of the Episcopal Church when a number of people believed that this had happened.

III

After teaching and chaplaincy work at Columbia University and an accomplished ministry as Dean of the Cathedral of St. John the Divine in New York City where his sermons, talks and writings vigorously addressed theological and ethical issues, James Pike became Bishop of the Diocese of California in 1958. Some saw this as an ideal post for a man with such a sharp and enquiring mind, eager to explore contemporary matters and to seek to make the Christian faith relevant to a changing world. Others were less sure, concerned that Pike might grow bored with the daily work of overseeing a diocese, and that the unevenness of aspects of his personality and his propensity to seek public recognition for his views might cause him problems.

There is no doubt that Pike wanted to call attention to what he was doing. Stories are still told in his diocese of the number of times he arrived late at large services and other gatherings. Some put this down to inefficiency on his part, but others saw it as a way of making known how busy and in demand he was and a way of heightening expectation for his arrival.

I recall being told by the editor of the diocesan paper in Chicago about how Bishop Pike would call her to ask what she thought was of interest and concern to the Chicago newspapers. In those days transcontinental flights often had to stop in Chicago, and Pike was prone to notify the press he was to be at the airport. There he would hold a press conference and often give his views in what he had been told was in the news before hopping on the next plane.

Pike, however, could be winsomely ingenuous about what he was doing. From his perspective he was accomplishing the job of a church leader, seeking to make the work of the Church and Christian perspectives known in an already secular age, and he was using the media to help do that work.

Pike had a deep and sincere desire to communicate what he understood to be the essential truths of the faith. He described himself as an existentialist rather than an ontologist, and it would likely be fair to say that he was more interested in the general human experiences of God and in ethics from a situational perspective than in special revelation. In this general stance he stood in a line which led from Schliermacher through Harnack, with the reformation in some measure behind them, looking for that which "is essential, absolute, unchanging about Christianity."[17] There was about him the spirit of the reformer, his voice raised when he held that any finalizing in theology of that which is less than ultimate could become the real blasphemy — the real heresy.[18]

Like many highly-intelligent theologians he wanted to simplify and to demystify in order, he believed, to enable the Church to reach those who were put off by too much dogma from the past and to make Christianity a more credible and effective force in the world. He once said of his book *If This Be Heresy?* that he had thought about calling it *Fewer Beliefs, More Belief*. One of his favorite images came from II Corinthians 4:7 where Paul speaks of having "this treasure in earthen vessels." Rather missing Paul's point, Pike wanted to make clear that the earthen vessels were not themselves the essential truths of Christianity.

"There are," he wrote in his 1964 book, *A Time for Christian Candor*, "many people within the fold who have not really grasped the heart of the Christian message because they are bogged down by too many doctrines, mores, precepts, customs, symbols and other traditions, with no sense of differentiation between the relative essentiality and non-essentiality of the respective items."[19]

"Many of us," he continued, "are convinced that theological reconstruction can bring more reality, conviction and consequent action, enabling more Christians to be more effective witnesses to Christ and His Church in the world."[20]

A good deal of what Pike wrote about may seem rather commonplace and perhaps unthreatening today. Rudolph Bultmann was still the leading New Testament theologian, and demythologizing was very much on the theological mind. There was no three-story universe with a heaven above and a hell below, no need for a devil or angels and so forth. What was important were the truths which could be found within mythological language.

Some of what Pike was after also seems quite minor. Archaic words like *vouchsafe, propitiation* and *succor* should be discarded. He made fun of what he called "fire worship," the quasi-ceremony over the extinguishing of candles at the conclusion of the liturgy. In many ways *A Time for Christian Candor* is a very churchy book, and one can tell that Pike was an active and involved bishop at the time of its writing.

But then there were larger issues. Pike was less inclined to talk in Bultmanesque terms about the resurrection, but he had often questioned any historical basis for the Virgin Birth. Indeed, pointing to the time-bound hellenized character of creedal language, he asked if it was not time for creeds to be rewritten. And, because the Greek and Latin ways of talking about God in terms of being, substance and persons were outdated and confusing, inclining, he feared, a number of Christians toward a kind of tritheism, it was time to rethink trinitarian language and theology.

In the way of human events, all the factors which led some bishops to want to bring Pike to ecclesiastical trial are not clear. Some of it probably had to do with personalities. There may have been jealousy of Pike's popularity with the media. Although an affable man in many ways, Pike's style was not very collegial, and he had ways of saying things which implied that those who could not view matters from his perspective were not wholly enlightened.

Yet there certainly were theological issues to be discerned as well. While few Episcopalians regard themselves as biblical literalists, there are a number who might be described as creedal "literalists" or who, at least, feel themselves to be rather literal about the truths they believe creedal language enshrines. And whatever language is used, trinitarian theology, not least in its understanding of the full divinity of Christ, stands at the heart of Christian faith.

As Pike himself sought to unfold his thinking, it does not appear that he was really, if at all, far from orthodoxy. He wanted to emphasize monotheism over any tendencies to tritheism and to avoid obfuscating language, but he could speak movingly of the transcendence of God, of God's immanent presence and the presence of God in Christ. Like other rationalizing theologians before him, Pike may have failed fully to understand that the Christian understandings of the trinity and the two natures of Christ did not first emerge from the work of theologians, but grew from worshipping, suffering, hoping and serving Christians who knew the Spirit present in their lives was of the transcendent creator God who had been present in the life, death and now the new life of Jesus, who also had to have lived a fully human life like theirs to be their savior. Logic cannot wholly comprehend this monumental belief, but faith may trust in it and then may try to understand.

Pike might have used some assistance with his theological articulation and perhaps more with his style (although he did also believe in the value of shocking people). For a time, it appeared that issues would come to a head, but Pike's personal problems and resignation, coupled with the careful pastoral work and the theological reflection of the Advisory Committee appointed by the Presiding Bishop, brought matters to a kind of conclusion, then sadly punctuated by Pike's somewhat bizarre (and, probably to his liking, well reported) accidental death.

As the Report, with its accompanying Advisory Papers, wrestles with the questions regarding whether there can be heresy in the contemporary Church and what could be its character and a proper response to it, there emerges a kind of consensus regarding what alone would be threatening to the very existence of the Church by striking at the "existential reality of the Church's distinctive life." In the words of John Knox, quoted by the Report,

> ... thus reality can be expressed only in the terms in which it has been expressed from the beginning — the rich, concrete terms of the New Testament and of the Church's devotional literature — terms like the love of God, his truth and grace, his self revealing action in the history to which the Church belongs and of which its own creation is the center; the redemption in Christ, human and divine, crucified and risen, a redemption from both the guilt of sin and its power; the new life in the Spirit, rich in joy and peace and hope, the earnest of an everlasting inheritance.[21]

In its irenic stress on the essentials of the faith, the Report takes a kind of minimalist position with respect to doctrine which in its own way reflects a reformation attitude and a spirit deep in Anglicanism which wishes to be insistent only about those things necessary to salvation. There is far more an emphasis on the center of faith than on limits to diversity.

In this the Report presages the opinion from the trial of Bishop Walter Righter (who had ordained deacon a gay man in a committed relationship) with respect to the doctrine of the Church. Neither of these discussions, however, answers all our questions or can be regarded as wholly satisfactory, while they do delineate a profoundly catholic insight echoed also in the Episcopal-Lutheran Concordat which, after years of conversation, study and prayer, brings these churches to "recognize in each other the essentials of the one catholic and apostolic faith."[22] In other language Richard Norris speaks of the unity of the Church to be found in its essential "identity and calling" in the death and resurrection of Christ and rooted in "the apostolic witness" apprehended "through the original Gospel, the *Kerygma* that is on the one hand incorporated in the Scriptures and, on the other, reiterated as faith's confessional response in the baptismal symbol."[23]

The 1967 Report of the Advisory Committee goes on to make some recommendations regarding the need for openness and theological reflection in the Church and freedom of conscience and speech, which latter language may particularly reflect the time in which the Report was written. There are specific suggestions regarding the need for more education on the part of all Christians, a stress reflective of John Macquarrie's reminder that the "only real corrective for bad theology is better theology,"[24] and of Karl Rahner's admonition that it is through the teaching office rather than administrative means, and "the positive formulation of the true doctrine that error is really supplanted."[25] In wonderfully Anglican fashion, the Report points to the theological importance and the unifying character of the liturgy and in this context can be heard to offer its primary judgment:

> When Episcopalians are questioned about the supposed orthodoxy or heterodoxy of one of their members, their most likely response is to ask whether or not he wishes — sincerely and responsibly — to join them in the celebration of God's being and goodness in the prayers and worship of the Prayer Book.[26]

The Report recognizes some problems with this test of orthodoxy, but concludes that only if a person "feels he cannot [join in this worship and identity with the *Book of Common Prayer*], then he should acknowledge that he can no longer function as an authorized officer or teacher of the Church."[27]

IV

Questions remain for us, along with issues for study and debate. Diversity in human nature being what it is, some people are more tolerant and are even appreciative of a certain untidiness in church teaching and order than others. There is, of course, a need in any effective community for both order, definition and identity, on the one hand, and room for change, creativity and new understanding on the other.[28] And there is bound to be tension between them. Clearly, however, over the years the Episcopal practice has been to allow for and value a rather large measure of freedom in thought and practice — finding unity for the Church in the common worship (even with some considerable diversity of form in that) and in a consensus, if not always sharply defined, around the core of the faith as embodied in the central stories of the Scripture and their repeated themes then set forth in liturgy, creed and sacraments.

While there can be risks in such an approach or way of belief and practice, it does tend to put the focus on God and the experience of God's presence. It assumes that this is what faith is primarily about — less the answers to life's questions than the direction in which a relationship with the Source and Spirit of all life is to be found.

In one sense this puts less weight on the teaching office, for there is no large body of definition to be passed on. Yet at the same time it becomes more important that the shaping character of the formative stories and the core understanding of the faith, the practice of prayer and worship and living in a community of faith are taught and imparted. Where there is more scope for communities and individuals to make choice in their response to God's call in Christ to holiness and service, there is a greater need to help people gain the Christian wisdom and guidance which will enable them to speak out faithfully and to grow toward "maturity, to the measure of the full stature of Christ" (Ephesians 4:13).

This more open *way* of faith calls for great trust in the Spirit of God more than in an institution and its ability to guide and protect. Nor need the institution devote its time in trying to defend God or its understanding of God and God's ways. There is rather an assurance and reconciliation in the faith that God stands behind and within the human adventure and is faithful and lasting in love's justice and mercy.

Nor need there be anything tentative about this way. One can be firm in faith and yet properly modest in theology. Indeed, there is much to be learned from many of the great saints and teachers of the faith which suggests that the two go together — that it is a proper humility about what is not surely known in human life and a faithful wrestling with difficult theological and moral issues which allows greater space for the Spirit of God in life.

A model for me, and I know for many others in this appreciation of the way, has been Desmond Tutu. Possessed by the core drama of Christianity, firm in faith and unyielding in opposition to the wrongs of apartheid, racism, and oppression, the focus of this teacher and the direction he offers to others is toward God. And with this, in spite of all the suffering and evil he has seen and experienced, there is acceptance of others, compassion and mirthfulness. I know that Desmond, too, has had his times of doubt and darkness, but he has great trust in God and Jesus which brings a joy to his life and ministry, and frees him from the kind of rigidity and anger that otherwise comes from thinking it is our job to defend God or the Church.

It is this core faith which all teachers, and perhaps especially bishops, are to know, to be possessed by and be able to share and interpret. It forms the foundation for faithful belief and living. Other things may be valuable for Christian living; other things may be added to the structure, but they must, as it were, fit upon that foundation — a foundation which will always be discernably cruciform. And in the spirit of an always reforming Christianity, there should be something regularly probing and testing in our use of what is built on that foundation, recognizing how even what was once valuable may change, how acculturated our ways often are, and how new understanding and the Spirit can move the Church.

In a discussion of development and continuity of the Church's tradition, Bishop Michael Nazir-Ali reflects on the "once-for-allness" of the faith and yet the need for "each generation, each culture, each community" to receive the "faith afresh."[29] He offers three principles for the development of the faith.

"First, genuine development must conserve the core of the Gospel tradition — not everything in it, but the core of it." Scripture is the normative part but "not everything in Scripture is the core." "There ought," he goes on, "to be continuity between the doctrine, or the practice that has developed, and the core of the tradition." The second principle calls for "engagement with the present ... profound engagement with our state of knowledge, with the concerns people have...." And, thirdly, there should be "acceptance of the future" — a recognition that Christianity, linked to its past, is always open and oriented to God's future.[30]

Teaching and interpreting the core faith, discerning the continuity, engaging with present knowledge and understanding, openness to the future — these are all vital aspects of the teaching ministry of the Church, the work of *episkope* in which bishops have a distinctive role to play. And, as we have continued to see, a role not without the experience of tension, although potentially always a creative tension in the life of faith.

Eric Mascall, in his contribution to the *Report of the Advisory Committee* dealing with the Pike situation, seems to come down on one side of the tension (and may have been directing his remarks at Pike) when he wrote: "The function of the bishop as a guardian and teacher of Christian truth should be emphasized, and any suggestion that he is simply a gifted thinker who has been given prominence in order to disseminate his own original ideas should be clearly repudiated."[31] One recalls from that time others who said it was permissible for Pike to express some of his views and questions when he was a teaching theologian or even as a prominent cathedral dean, but, if he wished to continue to do this, he should not have become a bishop. Yet, one could also ask, what would happen to the overall *episkope* teaching ministry of the Church if all bishops emphasized the guardian role of their office in such a way that the faith was preserved yet not also boldly proclaimed and interpreted? Would that, we ask again, be faithful to the tradition?

It is helpful here to recall Cyprian who, in emphasizing the unity of the Church and the role of bishops in that unity, maintained that "the episcopate is a single whole, of which each bishop has a right and responsibility for the whole."[32] While Christianity is now divided into many communions and churches, and, even in the Anglican Communion bishops from around the world meet only every ten years, each bishop may still share in the understanding that he or she is part of a larger, on-going apostolic ministry with no right simply to have one's own version and interpretation of the faith. Yet it is also true that bishops are given different gifts and that they find themselves in a variety of cultural circumstances. Unity need not and probably had best not require only one voice, but might speak, as do the Gospels, with some different emphasis and concerns, setting forth and interpreting the same core faith. Indeed, that could well be heard as a richer corporate voice and, for evangelical purposes a richer form of unity.

For there to be this richer unity several things, however, remain necessary. First, bishops need to have, not only a profound knowledge of the core faith, but also understanding of how and why it is so shaped and of the interpretations given to it in the past. Their teaching and theological reflection cannot be effective and well respected without being part of that continuity.

Secondly, they should be in regular dialogue and conversation with others. This need not mean full agreement on all issues, but it does involve consultation and learning from other bishops — sharing in the episcopate. It means being also in dialogue with the people and other clergy of their diocese — listening as well as teaching. Indeed, one could maintain that the Church's best theology was always percolated up rather than being issued in some top-to-down manner. This certainly does not mean every voice is equally perceptive or that it is always the majority voice that is wisest. But the mind of Christ speaking through the Spirit in the Church emerges through the faithful prayer and service, the suffering and the endurance of those seeking to be of Christ's body in the world.

Searching for the mind of Christ asks for a bishop's understanding of and participation in the concerns of others, the concerns of the society, the hearing not just of prominent voices but of minority and sometimes marginalized voices, (including voices marginalized in the tradition), being able sometimes to speak for them to others. That can be challenging and prophetic work, but not to do so could well mean a failure to conserve and carry forward the faith of Christ.

There is tension again. The bishop is conservator but also an agent of change and new understanding if the faith is to be preserved. Respecting the tradition and institution, the bishop is also called to be among its prophets, helping others to see what they otherwise might not and might prefer not to see, not only in the society about them but in the Church itself: racism, self-serving, unfairness, hypocrisy, apathy, poverty, neglect. Forms of near-superstition and wishing to use religion like magic may be disguised as piety. Nineteenth-century understandings of natural law and theology may present themselves as part of the eternal order. Distorted Christologies can be said to be the simple faith. Loyalty to clan, class or country may deeply color faith.

Truth should always be spoken in love, but the faith cannot be guarded and preserved unless one also tries faithfully and boldly to proclaim and interpret it. No bishop, of course, or group of bishops will do this teaching ministry perfectly, but the Gospel is best heard, not in some faultless presentation, but in the faithful trying.

V

With my tongue a bit in my cheek (since George Bush was then saying he wanted to be "the education President") I told my diocese that I wished to be its "education bishop." We have made education for all one of our three diocesan priorities, understanding it not just as head knowledge, but as Christian formation as well, learning how to pray, do stewardship, worship and serve in ministry along with knowing the core faith and its basic theology and gaining insight into Christian ethics and their living. The bishop was and is to play a leading role.

Over the past decade I have learned how important this education is for ministry (the good evangelism and ministry and shared understanding which take place when it is present; the opportunities missed when it is not) but also how hard it is to do. Sentimentalism about religion, driving a kind of anti-intellectualizing suspicion of tradition and authorities, a seeping deconstructionism, these are probably all part of the mix in which all of us seek to minister. I also hear from many of the clergy, and feel and see for myself, the running complaint, "people just don't have enough time." The busyness of modern life (generated probably as much by the plethora of options and information and entertainment sources as by what must be done) squeezes if not eliminates more traditional opportunities for Christian education. Mix this with this the predominately secular character of so much education and media, and one finds that even many bright and active disciples can have a rather thin veneer of faith knowledge and understanding.

Countering strategies can be devised. The sermon can be a teaching opportunity, particularly when it is intentionally and regularly employed in this way. Videos, audiotapes, and various print presentations can be used for individual learning as well as with groups in a variety of formats. We have relearned what good educational understanding teaches — that much of the best learning takes place around preparing for new ministries: in baptismal and confirmation classes (especially when they can be made into a form of catechumenate), when becoming a lay reader, lay eucharistic minister, church school teacher, catechist, Stephen minister and so forth. We have had some of our best success with the Education for Ministry program. Less often, but with interesting results, have been efforts to reflect on the faith aspects of vocations, like those in teaching and in medicine.

We do not in this space have the opportunity to explore all the challenges and opportunities which are available for Christian learning and teaching today. But bishops can begin again with themselves. First of all, there is the learning and preparation which one gains before becoming a bishop. Not everyone will have the charism it takes to be a fine teacher, but probably no one should become bishop unless he or she has the learning to do so and the desire to teach. Few bishops today come from a background as professional theologians, but all interpreters are theologians and each can be as thoughtful as he or she can be.

Time pressures are severe on bishops, too, and, sadly, there is rarely a constituency clambering for the bishop's time for study, prayer, reflection, and to meet with other theologians, to read and discuss books together, and do other forms of continuing education. So the time and opportunities must often be fought for, seized upon, created. One has the reward not only of the learning and insights, but of being a model of their importance to others. It is good for the Church whenever bishops can do this together.

And then there is the challenge of finding opportunities to teach as a bishop today. In many dioceses, the bishop may be seen as a rather distant, not well-known figure. And there are many other responsibilities.

Nor may teaching with one's own clergy be easy when they can share in many of the same cultural circumstances mentioned earlier. But there are opportunities: of course, Sundays and other preaching occasions, videos and articles and letters, from time to time (perhaps especially in crises of one kind or another) through the secular media, teachers' gatherings, smaller and larger clergy meetings, with groups of lay leaders who can be called together, in one-on-one situations, conventions, stewardship conferences. At least several times a year, one can accept invitations to teach in congregational programs.

Nor need one always be the only or lead teacher. One can teach and learn with others and invite others to come and teach and reflect together. The challenges and the tension, but also the opportunities continue — all of them together making it as important as ever that bishops give their best effort to the ministry of teacher and theologian.

NOTES

[1] Augustine, *City of God* 19:19. See J. Robert Wright, "The Origins of the Episcopate and Episcopal Ministry in the Early Church" pp. 10-32 in *On Being a Bishop: Papers on Episcopacy From the Moscow Consultation 1992.* Ed. Wright (New York: Church Hymnal Corp. 1992), p. 12.

[2] See Wright in *On Being a Bishop*, pp. 16-20.

[3] Irenaeus, *Against Heresies*, 3:3:1.

[4] See "The Ministry of Bishops: A Study Document Authorized by the House of Bishops of the Episcopal Church," pp. 78-106 in *On Being a Bishop*, pp. 80-81. The first of the three sections of this Study is "The Bishop as Proclaimer and Teacher," pp. 84-91.

[5] *Episcopal Ministry: The Report of the Archbishop's Group on the Episcopate 1990* (London: Church House Publishing, 1990), Section 55, p. 24.

[6] Charles P. Price, "Teachers and Evangelists for the Equipment of the Saints. Prayer Book Doctrine Concerning the Bishop as Teacher, Evangelizer and Focus of Unity," pp. 107-128 in *On Being a Bishop*, p. 111.

[7] Concordat, paragraph 3.

[8] "Baptism, Eucharist and Ministry," M29.

[9] Journal of the General Convention, 1982, pp. C-56 and 57.

[10] Paul D. Hanson, *The People Called: The Growth of Community in the Bible* (San Francisco: Harper & Row, 1986.)

[11] See my brief discussion of this in "All Things Necessary to Salvation" in *Anglicanism and the Bible*, ed. F. H. Borsch (Wilton, Conn.: Morehouse-Barlow, 1984), p. 206 with reference to W. H. Kelber, *The Oral and Written Gospel: The Hermeneutics of Speaking and Writing in the Synoptic Tradition, Mark, Paul and Q* (Philadelphia: Fortress Press, 1983).

[12] For a discussion, see Mark William Worthing's *God Creation and Contemporary Physics* (Minneapolis: Fortress Press. 1996), pp. 73-110.

[13] For a penetrating discussion see Robert J. Schreiter, *Constructing Local Theologies* (New York: Orbis Book, 1985).

[14] *Theological Freedom and Social Responsibility: Report of the Advisory Committee of the Episcopal Church.* Stephen F. Bayne, Jr. Chairman (New York: Seabury Press, 1967), p. 8.

[15] *Ibid.*, p. 19.

[16] In "A Will to Community," pp. 111-116, one of the contributed papers in *Theological Freedom and Social Responsibility*, p. 111.

[17] James A. Pike, *A Time for Christian Candor* (New York, Evanston, London: Harper & Row, 1964), p. 58.

[18] See *Christian Candor*, pp. 24-25.

[19] *Christian Candor*, p. 9.

[20] *Christian Candor*, p. 10.

[21] *Report*, pp. 23-24.

[22] *Concordat*, paragraph 2.

[23] Richard A. Norris, Jr., "Bishop, Succession and the Apostolicity of the Church," pp. 52-62 in *On Being a Bishop*, pp. 52-53.

[24] John Macquarrie, "Some Thoughts on Heresy," pp. 37-46 in *Report*, p. 43.

[25] Karl Rahner in his essay on "Heresy" in *Inquiries* (New York: Herder & Herder. 1964), p. 458 quoted by Macquarrie, *op. cit.*, p. 44.

[26] *Report*, p. 21.

[27] *Report*, p. 21.

[28] See my discussion " Freedom and Form" in *Outrage and Hope: a Bishop's Reflections in Times of Change and Challenge* (Valley Forge, PA.: Trinity Press International, 1996), pp. 79-81.

[29] "Development and Continuity," pp. 1-2 in *Affirming Catholic News* (No. 5, Feb. 1996), p. 1.

[30] The above quotations are all from "Development and Continuity," p. 2.

[31] Eric L. Mascall, "Orthodoxy, Heresy and Freedom," pp. 80-96 in the *Advisory Report*, p. 95.

[32] *De Unitate 5.*

A Church Bruised
and Changed

John Elbridge Hines, 22nd Presiding Bishop of the Episcopal Church from 1965 to 1974, died on Saturday, July 19, 1997. He was 87.

John Hines was born in Seneca, South Carolina, in 1910. His father was a doctor and a Presbyterian. His mother was an Episcopalian, and through much of his childhood John was influenced by both churches.

It was as an Episcopalian and a handsome, athletic young man that he matriculated at the University of the South at the age of sixteen. Always a warm and an engaging person, he naturally held leadership positions there and at the Virginia Theological Seminary from which he graduated before he was yet twenty-three years old.

Service as curate with a congregation in St. Louis, then with a smaller congregation in Missouri, followed by larger congregations in Augusta, Georgia, and then Christ Church in Houston, Texas, were part of John Hines's learning and rapid rise to prominence in the church. At the age of thirty-four he was elected Bishop Coadjutor of the Diocese of Texas, assuming more and more Episcopal responsibilities until he became diocesan in 1955 at the age of forty-four.

In a period of much church attendance and growth, Bishop Hines was a builder of new congregations and the new seminary in Austin. Calling himself a "liberal evangelical" or "theologically conservative but socially progressive," he pushed hard for integration in his diocese. Foreshadowing his years as Presiding Bishop, he found as a result that funding for the Diocese was sometimes withdrawn or withheld, and he was criticized for stretching resources too thinly.

There was always about Hines, however, an ability to deal with criticism when he felt gospel issues were at stake. When people asked him where he found his mandate for calling the church to deal with issues of prejudice, racism and poverty, he replied simply, "the Bible."

Dogged over the years by those who contended that evangelism and spirituality should be priorities over social responsibility and action, Hines refused to believe these priorities could be separated from one another. Not above feeling the pain of criticism and personal attacks, he nevertheless was seemingly without vengefulness or spite. John Coburn once said of him, "In all the years I worked closely with him, I never — despite what I considered many provocations — never heard him say an unkind or malicious word about anyone."

His personal kindness, his inner strength and gospel convictions, perhaps along with his southern connections, where the Episcopal Church has long been strong, were important reasons for Hines's somewhat surprising election as Presiding Bishop to replace the ailing Arthur Lichtenberger. Stephen Bayne had been the odds-on favorite, but was perhaps thought of by some to be too cerebral, too much of an elitist, perhaps too liberal and too connected with national church organizations. A majority of bishops, a number of them from more conservative dioceses, likely thought Hines to be the safer candidate.

What propelled Hines's years as Presiding Bishop into controversy were the civil disturbances and rioting in several of America's cities during the summer of 1967 and the response of the General Convention in Seattle of that year and of the Special Convention held in South Bend in 1969. Hines's own first response was to tour the affected areas and to listen. Through that listening and from his own earlier experience, the relatively new Presiding Bishop became convinced that a dramatic response was necessary. He brought to the Seattle Convention a program, to become known as the General Convention Special Program, which would take millions of dollars from regular church activities and allocate them to ecumenical and non-church programs working in the inner cities. A key word was empowerment and Saul Alinsky's principles of community organization provided one of the primary models. It was felt that it was important to avoid forms of paternalism, the largely white church telling blacks and others where and how to spend the money to help build up their communities and institutions. To the South Bend Convention, each diocese was asked to bring as extra representatives a woman, someone less than twenty-five years of age and a minority person. This was clearly an effort to influence the character of the debate and the power balance in the Episcopal Church.

Hines's prophetic theology and leadership were critical for the approval of the GCSP, but far from everyone was convinced of its purposes and opposition continued to grow. From the first, there were bishops and others who felt the GCSP violated the principles of diocesan rights which would allow dioceses and their bishops to determine which programs should be supported in their dioceses. Hines had argued that adherence to these rights could keep GCSP-supported activities out of the more conservative dioceses. In this he was surely right, but it left the door open to constant criticism of the Special Program, particularly when it was suspected or inferred that groups or individuals associated with GCSP activities were connected with violence.

Even more difficult to deal with were criticisms from Black-American Episcopalians who still found the GCSP to be a sophisticated form of paternalism and who likely felt that they, who often themselves felt powerless in the Episcopal Church, were now being bypassed in the decision-making and the organizations as grant recipients.

Most troublesome, however, were continuous attacks on the management and supervision of the Special Program. Such criticisms are, of course, a favorite means of those who oppose a program in their efforts to curtail or undermine it. But there was also a good deal of ammunition. Hines had chosen Leon Modeste to direct the program. Modeste was himself more interested in the principles of empowerment and more skilled in seeing opportunities than in careful direction and supervision. Hines's own style led him to give complete support to Modeste and to defend him and the program from criticism.

Yet, whatever the failings of the GCSP, vital new initiatives were developed and sustained to bring opportunity and leadership into impacted communities. Despite the aspects of the program which needed improvement, Hines continued to be regarded by many within and outside the

Church as a prophet and a man of great courage. The Episcopal Church was undergoing at least a measure of transformation. Hines himself said that he "hoped the GCSP would save the church's soul. It was to show that the church had at least a partial understanding of what the cross meant."

Early in 1973, John Hines installed me as dean of the Church Divinity School of the Pacific where one of his sons (three of them were to become priests) was then a student. Shortly afterward I found myself on an after-dinner program with him speaking to a group of Episcopalians at a country club in Phoenix. I was a small player in that evening's presentation and probably saw it as my job to make some complimentary references about God and the assembled group and to make a pitch for support of the seminary. John Hines was there to tell it as he saw it from a prophetic gospel perspective to an increasingly thin-lipped audience. On this and other occasions, he would say that none of us could "with humility receive the Sacrament of the broken body and poured blood of Christ while [anyone is] denied access to decent housing and jobs and the right to self-determination because of the oppressive character of political and social structures in which we find it convenient to acquiesce."

When challenged about charges that the GCSP had sometimes allied the church with people associated with violence, he would reply:

> ...violence is not simply all on one side, not simply on the side of what we call the oppressed people who are fouled up on their own life and the people who want to take it out on society. That much of violence is built into our normal structure. And unless we understand this and learn to change these structures, then the structures continue to do violence to people all through the whole range of our society. Violence comes out of frustration and rage on the part of people, individuals and also corporate groups.

Asked about the church losing members because of stances he had taken, the bishop would reply:

> I think it's a risk the church must take. You can't just play the antiseptic game all the time. If we really believe that Jesus Christ is Lord for us and we watch Him, then we find out that

he was not very much concerned for His own welfare, you see. He certainly wasn't concerned for his own reputation in the community. And more frequently than otherwise, he was found, according to some people, consorting with those whose reputations were quite bad. And yet his concern for them, nonetheless, was redemptive. And I think the Church has to emulate this... and let the chips fall where they may.

During the ten years John Hines was Presiding Bishop the national church staff, because of the diversion of monies to the GCSP and the withholding of funds by dioceses, congregations and individuals, was reduced by two-thirds. The church may have lost more than a million members. Almost all the loss of membership took place during that period for, since 1974, the number of people actually worshipping in Episcopal churches has somewhat increased.

Not all the loss is to be explained as due to Hines or the General Convention Special Program by any means. Demographics also played an important role as did the increasing secularization of society. Going to church was less necessary for social approval, and it became clear that many people had not been very well discipled during the growth years of the '50s. There were other changes taking place as well. Under Hines the Episcopal Church began to take social responsibility in investing and was one of the early supporters of divestiture in South African investments. Women delegates were seated at the General Convention and the ordination of women was clearly on the horizon. Liturgical experimentation and revision, which would lead to a new *Book of Common Prayer*, were begun. The Vietnam War, although Hines was not one of the early critics, was being opposed by many within the Episcopal Church.

Much of this change would have happened without John Hines and would take place sooner or later, if a bit less dramatically, in other denominations. But it was clear that John Hines boldly and unflinchingly led the way and that a number of people who had probably valued the Episcopal Church as a haven for what they regarded as conservative societal and political values were, at the least, unhappy.

If one believes God chose John Hines to lead the Episcopal Church during this period, one can once again be surprised by the people God chooses. At least on the face of it a man from South Carolina and Texas may not have seemed like the one to help lead the church in the battle against segregation, racism and unfair and oppressive structures in society — unless perhaps one knew his doctor father and mother caring for so many people in South Carolina and the young man who had taken his own gospel preaching so much to heart.

Hines's administration and his legacy are certainly open to criticism. If he was going to start something as significant as the General Convention Special Program, he probably needed to pay closer attention to its implementation and the people running it. Maybe he should have spent even more time bringing others along and hearing the criticisms of the Program, although time was also of the essence, and it is all too easy for an institution like the church, trying to please many people, to become paralyzed in a crisis. Probably even more to the point, was the challenge of dealing with a church where the real power and authority is in the congregations and to a lesser extent the dioceses. Trying to convert the grass roots from above is always hard.

In many ways the critics won. The GCSP became more limited and diluted as time went on. At the end of Hines's time as Presiding Bishop, the Program was pretty much finished. The House of Bishops saw reason to elect the most conservative of the candidates as Hines's successor. The Vietnam War was ended. Gradualism and local charitable activities became the policy in matters of racism and poverty. Other issues came to dominate.

Yet clearly the Episcopal Church was not the same. Hines had helped to convert some to his vision, and others had been drawn to a church concerned with social justice and issues. Some who opposed such concerns or who just didn't want to be part of such a church had left. But even one of Hines's strongest critics, who worried about the short term harm that has been done to the church, said, "the long term results of Bishop Hines's leadership will be good for the church. I think that very many Episcopalians are ashamed of our lethargy in social matters."

John Hines wanted to be part of a church which might have to survive, as he put it, "bruised, changed [but] also renewed." Throughout his ministry he was guided and strengthened by his prayer life and a conviction that what was most important was to concentrate on the Lordship of Jesus and the principle teachings of the gospel.

This was his own prayer which he often used:

> God, grant us a right discernment
> between that which comes first in our faith
> and that which follows after.
> And when we would make much of that
> which cannot matter much to thee,
> recall us to the heart of our Christian profession,
> which is Jesus Christ — Lord.

Going On

One day tricky Dick, then old Frankie boy,
and, of course, there was dad, and down the street
that sweet gal I but gabbed with now and then,
followed by grit and grin Burt Lancaster,
which makes me, for some reason, think of Kate
"God Bless America," and on the steps
of our Abraham, no less, "My Country
'Tis of Thee," sung so proud and hauntingly.
Bless Marian Anderson and Satch Paige
who knew you sometimes win and sometimes lose,
while on other days you just gets rained out.

I knew them all, at least it seemed I did;
that includes the three kids mashed from life
in the head-on crash on route forty-five.
I saw that on the news a while ago,
with all of them that went down on that plane.
Before them Cesar Chavez and the guy
who sold me vegetables and my newspaper,
whose way of looking down and up at you
reminded me of my science teacher,
who must be gone. And the amazing thing
is that any of us are still around;
I mean we all die, but it's if and when
one tries to think on it, I realize,
that it's because we all go one by one,
or in little clumps that living seems not
to notice or change that much, managing
to go on, which is good, and somehow strange.

What Do You Pray For?

What do you pray for? I find this one of the most interesting and revealing questions about the spiritual life. Sometimes, the question produces guilt. Gee, I don't pray enough. Or, I don't think much of what I pray about.

But those are just preliminary responses, perhaps in part defensive gestures to avoid talking about what may seem too intimate. We may also suppose that what we pray for isn't important enough, or that it is too mundane or trivial or even wrong. Lord, I pray to win the lotto only this once. It should solve almost everything, and then I'll be better able to serve you. One remembers the joke: "When I was little and didn't know any better, I prayed for a new bicycle. Now that I'm more mature, I pray for a Mercedes."

I have, however, learned something important about prayer — and that is not to leave out the things one really wants. Prayer cannot be honest if love is on my lips and the lotto in my heart. One of the things I have always valued in the Psalms is the way the psalmist lets it all hang out — including getting even with one's enemies.

Such honest prayer may help us to gain a greater perspective on our deepest hopes and fears — what we most need and want. But it also brings up another problem. What do we really think God will do — or God can do — about our prayers? Scripture tells us that God is better than all earthly parents and will give good things to those who ask. That may often seem true, but we know, too, of prayers that do not seem to be answered. Sometimes they are the most desperate pleas to spare a loved one. And we may imagine all the prayers cried out in the midst of Holocaust. Do we believe that God can or will intervene in the world of automobile crashes,

AIDS, poverty and Intifada to answer our prayers for safety and cure, justice and peace? These are hard and perhaps confusing questions. We know that no squad of angels came to rescue Jesus from the cross. We hear his cry of forsakenness. Yet still he prayed.

Job, too, kept on praying — even when things seemed bleakest and God seemed nowhere to be found. So did Paul with his "thorn in the flesh" that would not go away despite his many prayers. So did the psalmist, even though "my eyes grow dim with waiting for my God."

Their persistence reminds us what most they longed for: "As a deer longs for flowing streams, so longs my soul for you, O God. My soul thirsts for God." Although the worst may come, what most they ask is to be in the presence of God: "Even though I walk through the valley of the shadow of death, I fear no evil; for you are with me." Paul's thorn is not taken away, but he hears, "My grace is sufficient for you, for power is made perfect in weakness."

There are days when we are grateful to have words for our prayers. I am particularly grateful to have the Lord's Prayer: to know that I do not pray alone when, by myself or with the community of faith, I ask for God's kingdom and God's will — God's ways — to come on earth as in heaven. We pray for life's daily bread and the true bread of life; that we may be forgiven as we are given grace to forgive others; that we will not fall in the great temptation to give up on God's Spirit or to give in to evil. We can be grateful for other prayers that help us to offer thanksgiving and love, to pray for forgiveness and courage and strength better to serve, to pray for others and for ourselves.

There will be times, however, when we are beyond the understanding that shapes our words. We are not sure what to pray for. Then we yearn for "the Spirit that helps us in our weakness; for we do not know how to pray as we ought, but the Spirit intercedes for us with sighs too deep for words." George Herbert says that "prayer is God's breath in man" — God's breath in us, yearning with our spirits.

When in Luke's Gospel Jesus tells us that God knows how to give gifts better than earthly parents, the gift the heavenly Father offers "is the Holy Spirit to those who ask." What better gift for myself and for others for whom I pray than the divine Awareness as the context for their awareness in life, for God's Spirit with theirs, for Presence in the valleys, with the thorns and crosses and the sacraments and joys of life.

Sometimes, when I am praying for others, a curious thing happens. They begin to levitate in my prayers. They come up off the ground, and I imagine I see them with their legs sort of dangling and their jacket flapping — in all their vulnerability. I can see them, as it were, all around, and I imagine that this is something like God sees them and holds them up. The author of the 14th century *The Cloud of Unknowing* tells us that "God, with the all-merciful eyes, sees not only who we are and have been but who we will be." Without knowing what other things to pray for others or for myself, I ask for us and all people to be held in that Spirit.

In that Presence, one may then also ask for what Paul calls the fruit of the Spirit: "love, joy, peace, patience, kindness, generosity, faithfulness, gentleness and self-control." What more could one desire for ourselves or others? In that same Spirit I have long cherished this prayer from the Gallican Sacramentary:

> *Grant your servants, O God, to be set on fire with your spirit, strengthened by your power, illumined by your splendor, filled with your grace, and to go forward by your aid. Give them, O Lord, a right faith, perfect love, true humility. Grant, O Lord, that there may be in us simple affection, brave patience, persevering obedience, perpetual peace, a pure mind, a right and honest heart, a good will, a holy conscience, spiritual strength; through Jesus Christ our Lord.*

What do you pray for?

Who's He Retiring?

Losing some sense of identity, losing close relationships with associates and colleagues and their support, losing an office, coming nearer to the end of life: there are inevitably anxieties and feelings of loss as one retires. For me, this means retiring from forty-two years of parish ministry, being a professor and teacher, a seminary president and dean, a university professor, chaplain and dean, a bishop. Much of my identity, sense of value and purpose are tied up in these roles and titles. I recall some years ago asking the recently retired president of the Prudential Insurance Company how his retirement was going. "I went from *Who's Who* to who's he? in six months," he shot back.

On the other hand, I also remember one of Charles Kuralt's *On the Road* programs when he was interviewing an older gentleman somewhere in mid-America; it might have been Nebraska. Kuralt asked him, "Tell me, have you lived here all your life?" The man mused for a moment and responded, "Well, not yet."

There is much to which to look forward. I am fortunate to anticipate continuing opportunities to offer ministry, to teach, which I love to do, to write and keep my hand in advocacy work for the less advantaged — perhaps in more hands-on ways. Some people tell me one can end up busier than ever in retirement, but I imagine being able to pick and choose a bit more — to fashion something of my own schedule, within more of my own commitments.

By some definitions, I suppose Barbara and I are far from rich, but we are so much better off than many others. We have little to fear financially in retirement, if we mind ours P's and Q's. We seem to have remarkably good health. I don't think I expected to be so well and vigorous at the age of sixty-six. There will be more time for family and friends, the next canoeing trip to Canada, to read and write poetry, for prayer, to assemble archives.

Still, one finds oneself musing about things not done — roads not taken — other things one might have done. But I would have to be churlish not be enormously grateful for family love, for work and ministry accomplished, for so many colleagues and friends over these years.

So I go on to "who's he?" But what a good question: Who am I? Who is Fred? Away from titles and full-time work that so defines us in our society, what things do I care about, which people, what do I enjoy, what will I worry about, how do I propose to use my time? At the heart of any vocation in life, I have always believed, is more than what a person does; it is the kind of person one becomes.

I remember when my father retired from almost fifty years of practicing law. Rube had always imagined he would keep going and only begin to taper off one day. He used to tell me about John Black who still came to the office most mornings at the age of eighty-five.

But macular degeneration struck Rube in his late sixties. Also, the practice of law was changing. He had been a Rhodes Scholar and was a distinguished lawyer who still had clients who trusted only him, but the firm took his full-time secretary away and then his office. Reading became difficult without a great deal of magnification. Rube was a hard worker, putting in long hours and often with intense, time-driven cases. Some people suggested he would die within a year of retirement.

Not at all. Rube retired to the kitchen table where he set up his magnifying glass and light and assembled the various projects he wanted to work on, mostly home improvements. On the table was the telephone for extended calls to repairmen, to friends and family, along with his cups of tea and the cigarettes he soon gave up. Legal and other advice were dispensed for free. With Pearl, he took trips to Alaska and Africa and to England to see friends. He worked in his yard. He again served on the vestry and did his best to usher at church. He ate chocolate-covered marshmallow cookies. He loved his children and grandchildren. It turned out that his real work all along had been people and relationships.

For a time Rube was our own Mr. Magoo. He bumped into closed doors and spoke to people who had left the room. He told my mother how to drive and still wanted to put the car in the garage until he took the side-view mirror off one evening. But he learned to accommodate and lived another dozen years, more sunny and content than I had known him before. I think there were ways in which he became even more who he was. I learned more from him in those years than all the others. I intend to remember.

No Better Thing

*Reflections with the clergy at their annual
renewal of vows during holy week*

Some vows are hard to keep. There are days when our promises to be
faithful in prayer and the study of scripture, to teach and make known
the reconciling love of God, to show compassion and to serve those in
need seem demanding. There are times when our vows to work together
and be bound in love, to be guided by the pastoral direction and leadership of our bishop, and to pattern our lives so that we may be wholesome
examples seem confining and difficult to bear. God's hopes and expectations of us, the expectations and needs of others — all sense of duty and
responsibility — these can weigh heavily upon us. Our burdens and yoke
are heavy. The priest and poet George Herbert used the collar as a sign
and symbol of that sense of confinement — love's surrender of our idea
of freedom to do whatever we want.

> *I struck the board, and cried, "No more;*
> *I will abroad . . . ."*
> *leave thy cold dispute*
> *Of what is fit and not; forsake thy cage*
> *Thy rope of sands . . . .*

There is, however, one promise — at the heart of our vows — that we
find easier to hold onto, even as we pray more fully to appreciate and live
out its significance. We are met in holy week to enact this promise.
Through our baptismal covenant the breaking of the bread is command-
ment and promise for every Christian: "Do this in remembrance of me."
Together "we celebrate the memorial of our redemption . . . in this sacrifice of praise and thanksgiving."

Deacons are vowed to a special ministry of servanthood to assist in the
ministration of this sacrament. Priests are called "to share . . . in the cele-

bration of the mysteries of Christ's body and blood." Bishops have prom-ised to "support all baptized people in their gifts and ministries, to nour-ish them from the mysteries of God's grace . . . and celebrate with them the sacraments of our redemption."

I am privileged to have done this in every church and on every altar of this diocese. I have lifted up the bread and wine in churches large and small, churches high and low, hundred-year-old churches, in wonderfully refurbished churches, and in many a new church and building that we have together dedicated. I particularly remember celebrating Eucharist for the first time on this altar in our new Cathedral Center and thinking of the myriad times and occasions it will be offered here down through the years and perhaps in centuries to come.

I have prayed for the Holy Spirit to sanctify these gifts at conventions, conferences and camps, out of doors and in, Sundays and weekdays, morning noon and evening, scheduled and impromptu, in hospitals and prisons, for the burial of our brothers and sisters, after earthquakes and in the midst of riots, at baptisms, confirmations, ordinations and the cele-brations of new ministries.

All of you here have shared many of these occasions with me, and each of you have your own stories to tell of all the holy places and times you have shown forth the body and the blood. Indeed, I look out and see a hundred of you with whom I have talked and prayed in the days before your ordination. We spoke of where and when and with whom you would first break bread and pour out the wine and say, "The gifts of God for the people of God. Take them in remembrance that Christ died for you and feed on him in your hearts by faith, and with thanksgiving." We reflected on the many ways these words and acts would affect all your ministry.

Since I first heard Dom Gregory Dix's meditation on the observance of the Eucharist, it has been in my thoughts at many a celebration.

Was ever a command so obeyed? For century after century, spreading slowly to every continent and country and among every race on earth, this action has been done, in every conceivable need, from infancy and before it to extreme old age and after it, from the pinnacles of earthly greatness to the refuge of fugitives in the caves and dens of the earth. Men have found no better thing than this to do for kings at their crowning and for criminals going to the scaffold, for armies in triumph or for a bride and groom in a little country church; for the proclamation of a dogma or for a good crop of wheat; for the wisdom of the Parliament of a mighty nation or for a sick old woman afraid to die...

"No better thing than this to do." Will Willimon tells a story of when he was a young Methodist pastor and one of his friends was a youthful Episcopal priest. One day the priest came rushing up to Will's house on his bicycle with the news that the horror of the bombing in Cambodia had begun. Thinking perhaps of some protest they might join in, Will worriedly asked his friend what he thought they should do. Still catching his breath, the priest suggested that they plan a Eucharist.

"No better thing than this to do." No better thing than break the bread and pour out the wine. "This is my body given for you." "This is my blood of the new covenant shed for you and for many for the forgiveness of sins." This is the love of God in Christ seeking reconciliation — a forever sign of God's presence in the beauty but also the passion and heartbreak of life so that we will know that whatever happens to us happens in God.

When in 1678 Native Americans led Louis Hennepin to the foot of Niagara Falls, the awed Franciscan missionary fell to his knees, unstrapped an altar from his back and said Mass. "No better thing than this to do."

Back through forty-one years of ordained ministry I remember the Christmas Eve when I first celebrated the Eucharist as a priest. I remember the chapel in the theological college where I taught in England, the odd chapel at the Church Divinity School of the Pacific with the congregation sitting on either side, the neogothic chapel at Princeton that seats two thousand, full on Easter, Baccalaureate and memorial services, with one or two at a weekday Eucharist. I remember many other chapels and churches and meeting halls in countries of the Anglican Communion — in Africa, Asia, Central and South America — in our companion dioceses.

I remember taking teenage acolytes into the wilderness of Canada and, on the sabbath, rolling over a canoe to be our altar. The sun would glint off the aluminum skin with the dents and scratches from rocks we had encountered and flecks of flinty sand from the beach below. The cool wind rustled in the pines and ruffled the lake while a chipmunk scurried among our feet and a hawk circled above. "This is my body and my blood." I had scraped a bit of mold from the slice of bread that we otherwise would have used for one of our peanut butter and jelly sandwiches.

Another time some of us decamped in a Pentagon hallway and celebrated the Eucharist with several of the military joining in. Or we linked arms on a freedom march and sang "Holy, holy, holy." We broke the bread again in a war-torn province of El Salvador. "Do this in remembrance of me." We held up the bread and wine for those who were going to protest for decent wages, and in communion with members of other churches our Eucharist broke through all barriers.

"No better thing than this to do." There will be a last time for me and for you when we say "in remembrance that Christ died for you," "and at the last day bring us with all your saints into the joy of your eternal kingdom."

"Was ever a command so obeyed?" What better thing to do? because from this flows all else. We know again what God has done for us. "Guilty of dust and sin" and, despite all our protestations and attempts to earn love, our servant Lord tells us to "taste my Meat" — that we are to "sit and eat." We are drawn into communion with our Lord and one another. Once again does the burden become easy and the yoke light. Forgiven, we are made holy and asked to share in God's compassion. We are invited to show forth in our lives the reconciling love of God in Christ in ministries of prayer and service. Then are all our vows renewed.